Building Your Wealth Portfolio:
Mastering Your Money Habits and Achieving Financial Security

Darrell S. Jordan

TABLE OF CONTENTS

CHAPTER 1:

THE FOUNDATION OF BUILDING WEALTH

Many people aim to become wealthy, yet doing so can frequently seem like an impossible undertaking. Avoid being seduced by get-rich-quick schemes and possibilities that seem too good to be true because they could lead you down a perilous path because achieving this objective requires patience, perseverance, and discipline.

The good news is that anyone can build and maintain money over time by using certain ideas and tactics. Also, your odds of success are increased the earlier you begin using these.

We've listed several important wealth-building guidelines below, including establishing goals and creating a strategy, investing in education and skills, managing debt, saving money, investing it, safeguarding your assets, comprehending the effects of taxes, and establishing a solid credit history. Each of these principles will be discussed in more detail in this article, along with how they might assist you in reaching your financial objectives.

1. Making Money

You should start earning money right away. Although it may seem simple, this stage is the most important for people who are just getting started. You've probably seen graphs demonstrating how little sums of money saved consistently and allowed to compound over time can eventually develop into substantial sums. But those graphs never address the fundamental question of how to start saving money in the first place.

Earned income and passive income are the two main methods of earning money. Earned money is earned from your job, whereas passive income comes from investments. Unless you have enough money to start investing, you might not have any passive income.

These inquiries may help you choose what you want to accomplish and where your earned income will come from if you are either starting a career or thinking about changing careers:

What interests you? By engaging in work that you enjoy and find meaningful, you will perform better, develop a career that will last longer, and increase your chances of financial success. Research revealed that more than 90% of workers stated they would exchange a portion of their lifetime earnings for a job with more significance.

What do you excel at? Consider your strengths and how you may use them to support yourself. What will be lucrative? Choose occupations that fit what you excel at and enjoy doing and will fulfill your financial goals. You may get started in the correct direction by taking these factors into mind.

Investing in your education and talents is a smart move if you want to increase your earning potential. Obtaining higher degrees, certifications unique to your sector, and training courses are all beneficial ways to increase your human capital.

2. Create a plan and establish goals.

What purpose will you give your wealth? Do you want to save money for your future—possibly an early retirement? Paying for your children's college tuition? Purchase a second home? Give away some of your money to charity. The first step in accumulating wealth is setting goals. You may make a plan to get there after you have a clear idea of what you want to accomplish.

Establish your financial objectives first, such as retiring early, purchasing a property, or paying off debt. Be precise about how much money you need to make each goal happen and when you plan to make it happen.

After deciding on your objectives, you need to create a strategy for accomplishing them. Making a budget to help you save more money, boosting your income through education or professional progression, or purchasing investments that will increase in value over time are some examples of how to do this. Your strategy should be practical, adaptable, and long-term oriented. Review your progress frequently, and adapt as necessary, to stay on course.

3. Save cash

If you spend all of the money you earn, you won't be able to develop wealth. Also, you should put saving enough money ahead of everything else if you don't have enough saved up to cover your immediate expenses (such as bills, rent, or a mortgage) or an emergency. Many experts advise having three to six months' worth of salary saved up in case such circumstances arise.

Consider making the following decisions to save more money for growing your wealth:

For at least a month, keep a record of your spending. A compact, pocket-sized notepad could work just as well for this, but you might wish to utilize financial software. Keep a record of every purchase you make, no matter how tiny; you'd be shocked where your money goes.
Trim the fat where you can. Organize your spending by needs and wants. Needs like

clothing, food, and shelter are clear. You should also include the cost of health insurance, auto insurance if you own a car, and life insurance if you have dependents. Many more expenses will only be wants.

Make a saving target. Try to keep to your budget once you've determined how much you can save each month. This does not imply that you must always be thrifty or live simply. Be free to reward yourself and occasionally spend (in a suitable amount) if your savings goals are being met. You'll feel better and have more drive to continue on your path.

Activate automatic saving. Having your company or bank set up an automatic transfer of a specific amount of each paycheck into a different savings or investing account is a simple way to save a specific amount each month. Similarly to this, you can contribute to your employer's 401(k) or other retirement plans by having money automatically deducted from your pay. Financial advisors typically advise making a minimum contribution to qualify for your employer's full match.

Discover savings with a good return. Search for savings accounts with the greatest interest rates and fewest fees to maximize the return on your funds. If you have the financial means to lock away your money for several months or years, certificates of deposit (CDs) may be an excellent choice for your savings.

But keep in mind that cost-cutting can only be done so far. You should consider measures to enhance your revenue if your costs are currently really low.

Setting a spending limit is one of the best strategies to ensure that you are saving enough money. Reduce your unneeded and extra expenditures and invest your savings instead.

4. Invest

The next step after managing to save some money is to invest it so that it will increase. Savings are crucial, but deposit account interest rates are often very low, and your money runs the danger of losing purchasing power due to inflation over time.

For new investors (or any investor, for that matter), diversification is probably the most crucial notion. To put it plainly, you should try to diversify your investment portfolio. That's because investments behave differently depending on the time of year. For instance, bonds may be offering strong returns if the stock market is experiencing a losing stretch. However, if Stock A is struggling, Stock B can be tearing it up.

Due to their extensive variety of investments in securities, mutual funds offer some built-in diversification. Additionally, investing in both a stock fund and a bond fund (or many stock funds and multiple bond funds, for example) as opposed to just one of each will result in better diversification.

Another generalization is that you can afford to take more risks when you're younger since you'll have more time to make up for any losses.

Different Investments

Risk and potential return on investments vary. They often have lesser potential returns the safer they are and vice versa.

Spend some time reading up on the different kinds of investments if you aren't already familiar with them. Despite the wide variety of exotic investments available, the majority of investors will choose to start with stocks, bonds, and mutual funds.

Shares of ownership in a company are represented by stocks. When you purchase stock, you become a minor shareholder in that business and gain the upside potential of both its share price and any dividends it may pay. Bonds are typically thought of as being less risky than stocks, but the risk associated with stocks can vary greatly from firm to corporation.

Bonds function similarly to the government or corporate IOUs. When you purchase a bond, the issuer pledges to return your funds, along with interest, at a later time. Bonds are often thought to be less risky than stocks, but with less upside potential. Bond-rating organizations award them letter grades to reflect the fact that some bonds are riskier than others.

Mutual funds are collections of securities, frequently consisting of stocks, bonds, or a mix of the two. Shares in mutual funds give you access to the entire pool. The risk of mutual funds varies as well, depending on the investments they make.

Moreover, exchange-traded funds (ETFs) are similar to mutual funds in that each share contains the entirety of a portfolio of securities. But, ETFs are listed on exchanges and are traded similarly to stocks. Some ETFs follow specific industry sectors, asset classes like bonds and real estate, or important stock indices like the S&P 500.

Be sure you have enough savings and money left aside to manage any unforeseen financial problems before you begin investing.

5. Safeguard Your Assets

You put a lot of effort into earning your money and building your fortune. The worst-case scenario might be to lose everything as a result of an unexpected tragedy. Your home could be destroyed by fire, you could incur damage and medical costs from a car accident, or you could lose out on future income due to an early death.

Because it offers protection from these and other dangers, insurance is an essential component of accumulating wealth. In the event of a fire, home insurance will rebuild your house and possessions, auto insurance will make you whole after a collision, and life insurance will pay your dependents in the event of an early death. Another sort of policy that will replace your income if you get hurt, sick, or otherwise incapacitated and unable to work is long-term disability insurance. Although insurance policies tend to cost more as you age, even young, healthy people should think about buying them. This means that purchasing life insurance now, even if you are 25 years old and unmarried, may be significantly more affordable than waiting until you are 30 years old, and have a partner, kids, and a mortgage.

6. Reduce the Effects of Taxes
Taxes can hinder your efforts to accumulate wealth and are frequently disregarded. Of course, as we earn and spend money, we are all

subject to income tax and sales tax, but our investments and assets may also be subject to taxation. Understanding your tax vulnerabilities and creating plans to lessen their effects is crucial.

Investing in tax-advantaged accounts is a simple approach to reducing your tax obligation. These accounts, including 401(k) plans, IRAs, and 529 college savings plans, have tax advantages that can increase your savings and lower your tax obligation. A typical IRA or 401(k) contribution, for instance, allows you to lower your taxable income and save money on taxes in the year you contribute. Additionally, because they grow tax-deferred, the effect will be less noticeable when you retire, and are more likely to be in a lower tax rate. You can grow and withdraw money from a Roth account without paying taxes on any of the income or profits since investment earnings in a Roth IRA or Roth 401(k) are tax-free.

Being careful with the time and location of your investments is another way to reduce taxes. You can benefit from the reduced long-term capital gains tax rate, which is typically lower than the short-term capital gains tax and income tax rates, by keeping investments for more than a year. Also, keep in mind the locations of various assets. If given the option, a tax-advantaged account like a Roth IRA should be used to hold an income-producing asset like a dividend-paying stock or corporate bond because these payments won't result in taxable events there. An investment in a growth stock that will solely result in capital gains (rather than income) may be more advantageously held in a taxable account.

Working with a certified public accountant (CPA) or other competent tax professional, such as an accountant, can help you stay on top of these developments and create a tax strategy that is suitable for your particular financial circumstances. You may create wealth more effectively and keep more of your hard-earned money over the long run by understanding the effects of taxes and implementing ways to reduce their impact.

7. Control Your Debt and Improve Your Credit

You'll start to see the value in taking on debt to finance different investments or purchases as your wealth increases. Use a credit card to make purchases to get points or incentives. Applying for a mortgage, a home equity loan for house upgrades, or an auto loan to buy a car are all options. Perhaps you'll need a personal loan to fund the launch of your business or an investment in someone else's.

Nonetheless, it's crucial to handle your debt responsibly because accruing too much debt could impair your efforts to accumulate money. Pay attention to your debt-to-income (DTI) ratio when managing your debt, and make sure that your monthly debt payments fit comfortably into your spending plan. To prevent paying exorbitant interest fees, you should also try to pay off high-interest debt, such as credit card debt, as soon as you can. Be cautious when using products with variable or adjustable interest rates, such as adjustable-rate mortgages (ARMs) or those with balloon payments, as changes in the economy or your situation could suddenly make those obligations impossible to pay off.

If you go into debt, it might hurt your credit score, and if you don't pay your debts, you could file for bankruptcy.

Keeping a High Credit Score
Long-term wealth growth and preservation depend heavily on establishing and keeping a high credit score. If you have a solid credit history and a high credit score, you'll benefit from lower interest rates and better loan terms, which can ultimately save you thousands of dollars in interest payments.

These are some essential actions you may take to keep a high credit score:

Punctually pay your expenses. Your payment history is one of the key elements that determine your credit score. You must be sure to pay your payments on time each time if you want to keep your credit score high. Even a few days of late payments can have a major negative effect on your credit score.

Maintain minimal credit utilization. Another significant aspect that influences your credit score is your credit usage, or how much of your available credit you are utilizing. You should try to keep your credit use below 30% of your available credit to retain a high credit score.

Keep an eye on your credit report. Checking your credit report frequently is a smart practice to ensure that all the data is accurate and current. There are many services available today that will provide you with a free credit report. It's critical to challenge any mistakes you notice on your credit report because they might have a negative influence on your credit score.

Try not to create too many new accounts. Your credit score may be somewhat lowered each time you apply for credit. Avoid creating too many new accounts quickly if you want to keep your credit score high. But, keep in mind that you risk having insufficient credit history if you don't use credit cards or if you don't have adequate credit lines open. Get a few credit cards and obtain a few loans, but do not go overboard.

You may maintain a decent credit score and increase your borrowing power over time by adhering to these guidelines and developing excellent credit habits.

Should I invest or pay off debt?
It normally makes sense to pay off high-interest debt before making investments if you have any, such as numerous credit card balances. Few investments ever yield returns as high as credit card fees. Once your debt is paid off, put that extra cash toward savings and investments. As much as you can, strive to pay off the entire sum on your credit card each month to prevent accruing interest.

How much cash is required to purchase a mutual fund?
Many mutual fund providers have varied entry-level investment minimums, frequently starting at around $500. You can typically invest less after that. Several mutual funds can waive their initial minimums provided you

agree to make a consistent monthly investment. Via a brokerage company, you can also purchase shares of mutual funds and exchange-traded funds (ETFs). Some brokerage companies don't charge anything to start an account.

An exchange-traded fund (ETF) is what?
Similar to mutual funds, exchange-traded funds (ETFs) are investment pools. One significant distinction is that they trade their shares on stock exchanges (rather than buying and selling through a particular fund company). They occasionally impose lesser fees as well. Also, you can purchase them through a brokerage company together with equities and bonds.

the conclusion
Even though schemes to become rich quickly occasionally may seem alluring, the tried-and-true method of accumulating wealth is via consistent saving and investing—and patiently waiting for that money to grow over time. Starting little is acceptable. Starting early and consistently is crucial. Make money, save it, and then wisely invest it. Insurance can help

you safeguard your assets while reducing your tax liability.

Understand that accumulating wealth is a process rather than a final goal. Throughout the road, celebrate your accomplishments and resist the urge to give up because of setbacks or difficulties. You can succeed financially and accumulate wealth over time if you have patience, discipline, and a clear understanding of your objectives.

Defining Wealth And Financial Security

What is monetary safety?
Financial security is the condition of having enough money to cover one's basic expenses, including those for food, clothing, housing, healthcare, and other living costs, to manage financial difficulties without endangering one's health, and to save money for future obligations.

Your ability to live comfortably and your sense of safety are both reflected in your financial security. When your finances are stable, you don't stress over not having enough money or the ability to pay your payments.

Feeling as though you don't have enough money
When you don't have enough money, it can cause stress in all areas of your life. You could feel guilty or humiliated about not being able to afford goods that other people can simply purchase. Not knowing if there will be enough money left over each month after covering all of your expenditures is difficult. It becomes even

more difficult if you have someone else who depends on your salary. If you've ever experienced it, you'll know that this feeling is not at all cozy.

We'll then discuss what you can do to ensure that this emotion never returns to you.
How to get there financially:

Pay off your debt
Put your cash in a high-yield savings account.
Determine your spending patterns.
Living within your means
Establish objectives for yourself.
Don't borrow just to brag
Work with a financial advisor or gain financial knowledge on your own
possess insurance
Establish an emergency fund.
Increase your wealth by investing

1. Pay off your debt
Debt relief is the first step in achieving financial security. You feel like a slave to your creditors when you are in debt. Once you're out, however, it feels like a weight has been lifted off your

shoulders, allowing you to devote all of your attention to making deliberate progress toward financial freedom.

2. Put your cash in a high-yield savings account.
It's crucial to start saving money as soon as you can and as much as you can. The more time you give your money to grow and compound over time, the sooner in life you start saving for retirement. You can save money on Cowrywise in a savings account where you can earn higher interest rates on your deposits than are provided by conventional banks.

3. Determine your spending patterns.
Determine your spending patterns. This entails setting up a budget, being aware of where your money is going, and being aware of what you can afford to buy. Consider spending some time learning how money leaves your account.

4. Living within your means
Limit your spending to less than your income. The usual human propensity is to drift toward a more opulent lifestyle as wealth rises. But, that is not a smart move from the standpoint of

financial security. It is advisable to invest that excess money in increasing your emergency, retirement, and savings accounts. Maintain focus on your financial objectives.

5. Establish objectives for yourself.
What do I want my financial condition to look like? is a good place to start. How much money do I need to feel secure financially? What makes me want financial stability? These are solid starting principles that ought to assist you in outlining a specific objective for yourself. And when you set goals, make sure to put them in writing and give them deadlines. That way, you'll be more likely to follow through.

6. Don't borrow just to brag
If you need to borrow money, it should be for an investment in your business or yourself—basically, something that could make you money or move you closer to your financial objectives. Don't try to fake a lifestyle you don't yet have to impress others by borrowing money. Nobody could care less.

7. Collaborate with a financial advisor or gain financial knowledge on your own

You develop a financial improvement strategy with the assistance of your financial counselor. They give you advice on the best ways to manage your money and personal finances. If you don't have the funds to hire one, though, you can invest the time to educate yourself on personal finance issues and the investment options that best suit your financial objectives. Putting money into oneself pays off in spades.

8. possess insurance

The primary purpose of insurance is to act as a financial buffer against life's uncertainties, hazards, and unplanned losses. Making ensuring you have insurance is one of the first steps toward achieving financial stability. You ought to have a variety of insurance policies, including life, health, auto, property, and travel insurance.

9. Establish an emergency fund.

Another way to think about an emergency fund is as insurance. Ensuring you have access to cash, serves as a financial cushion to keep you afloat through tough financial circumstances.

10. Increase your wealth by investing
Another crucial step toward financial security is investing. Through investing, you can increase your net worth. To accomplish this properly, you need persistence, the ability to conduct thorough research, financial analysis expertise, and the self-control not to panic sell when prices drop or become overly greedy when prices climb.

Choosing between financial stability and security
Long-term objectives include financial security. It's important to have enough money to buy the things you desire, not simply the necessities. On the other hand, achieving financial stability is a short-term objective; it entails having enough money to get by each day without worrying about how you're going to pay your rent or energy bills for the upcoming year.

Financial stability entails having a steady source of income and some emergency funds on hand, but it doesn't guarantee that one revenue stream will cover all of your expenses. Achieving financial stability becomes more challenging when unforeseen expenses like medical bills for you or dependent family members arise, for example, if your only source of income is a minimum-wage job.

To sum up

The assurance that you will always have money on hand in case you need it allows you to focus on other aspects of your life or spend time with friends and family. Financial stability is crucial.

These pointers will put you on the road to financial security. If you have any queries or ideas, let us know in the comments.

Understanding the importance of mindset in building wealth

The idea that only people with millions of dollars in their bank accounts qualify as "rich" may be the largest wealth myth.

Nothing is more false than it is.

You'll receive three different answers if you ask any three people to define riches.

You must think like the wealthy if you want to be wealthy. Set YOUR financial objectives first. For example, how much money do you hope to have in a year? In five years?

Do you have a number? Good.

You must adopt a wealth attitude if you ever hope to see a dime of that cash.

The human urge for wealth is unlike anything else, whether it's driven by the pursuit of material comforts, financial independence, or the freedom that comes with having a "large quantity of money."
The path to prosperity, however, is rocky and littered with myths.

Why is having a wealth mindset important?
When we take into account the soaring amounts of credit card debt, the fact that 60% of Americans live paycheck to paycheck simply makes matters worse.

175 million Americans actively use credit cards as of 2018. Most of these credit card users use their cards impulsively, spending money they don't have on things they don't need.

These actions cause severe debt cyclones that are challenging to exit.

The fundamentals of the wealth mindset—being able to accumulate riches—appear to be a forgotten skill.

How do mindsets work?
A mindset is a perspective that you have on the world. It can slightly change what you see and how you think about it, similar to a pair of sunglasses.

Your thoughts and decisions are influenced by your mindset, which consists of your beliefs, perceptions, and attitudes.

The success toolkit you have at your disposal should include a variety of mindsets. Like spectacles, they might make your route difficult to see or make the road ahead more clearly. You can stay on track with your financial objectives and look for opportunities to boost your earning potential by cultivating a positive wealth attitude.

What exactly is a wealth mindset?
If you look closely at the accounts of affluent people, you'll see a pattern:

A wealthy individual will hardly ever be able to attribute all of their fortunes to one singular miracle. They'll say that their thinking is the main driver of their success instead.

A wealth mindset is a combination of ideas, routines, and actions that distinguish affluent people from the rest of the population. Making the most of the money you do have will be facilitated by a wealth mindset.

Yet it's not always simple. Spending less, making prudent investments, and seeking out low-risk strategies to enhance financial position are all characteristics of a wealth mindset.

The good news is that anyone can acquire this mindset with a little perseverance.

A poor mindset is what?
A poor mindset is the opposite of a wealthy attitude. Most people with this "bad mindset" are unaware of it.

Poor mindsets include any of the following: believing that working for a living is wrong, that it can be accomplished without effort, that you'll never be able to escape your debt, or that you lack the necessary skills to boost your cash flow.

If you don't take steps to change your thinking, it will actively work against your financial goals and keep riches away from you.

1. Be persistent, and patient, and set goals.
Goal-setting pays off, as evidenced by the woman at the summit of the mountain.
Very few successful people acquired their money overnight. Building riches takes time.

Mark Zuckerberg didn't become a billionaire thanks to Facebook. Mark Zuckerberg put a lot of effort and attention into building Facebook and later enjoyed the rewards of his efforts.

Don't place your faith in dangerous "get rich quick" schemes in the hopes of becoming wealthy.

The typical wealthy person plans their finances 10 times longer than the typical middle-class person.

Choose how much you want to save each month. More essential, make sure you follow the strategy you develop for yourself and that it is realistic. A budget enables you to look at your spending and identify areas for cost-cutting or elimination. Making tough decisions during this process, such as switching to less expensive versions of things or forgoing all extravagances, may be necessary.

You have a larger risk of failing and giving up on your goal of becoming wealthy if you have a poor track record of saving and set a goal of saving 10% of your upcoming paycheck.

Why not begin with 1%?

Start small, develop the habit, and gradually increase your efforts.

2. Invest money now for the future.
The coins on the tree show that having a wealth mindset includes investing.
Most people believe that money cannot be made by itself, but can it? Your invested funds can grow dramatically over time thanks to the concept of compound interest.

Earning interest on interest results in compound interest. You will receive a percentage of interest on the total amount of money in the account, which includes the amount you made the previous year, each year that your money is invested.

You will earn more money in return the longer you let your account develop.

Bill Gates had a $9.3 billion net worth in 1994. In 2014, the man had an estimated net worth of $81.6 billion.

Not just Microsoft sales drove this ninefold gain in wealth. Michael Larson, the manager of Bill Gates' assets, drove it.

Wealthy people generally invest their money, and you don't have to do it by yourself. Either learn how to invest or seek assistance. There are many skilled and reliable advisors available.

The final word? It would be a mistake to leave all of your savings sitting in a bank account.

In the past, candy bars cost 5 cents each. Nowadays, it would be difficult to find a Snickers bar for less than $1.

Inflation is the term used to describe a steady rise in product and service prices over time. With time, it lessens the value of money as a medium of exchange.

When you're ready to use your nest egg, it will be worth a lot less if your investment strategy is to keep your money in a savings account for years on end.

Consider your investment options instead. 401ks and Roth IRAs are two popular investment vehicles.

You can contribute to a 401k either directly or through your employer as a retirement plan. Either you contribute money to it yourself each month, or a small sum is deducted from each pay period and invested in the stock market. Your money will continue to grow until you decide to access it in your golden years, and employers may match your contributions. You will pay income tax on it when you withdraw the money because contributions are made on a pre-tax basis — the money you put in can lower your taxable income for that year.

A Roth IRA, which is funded with after-tax money, is another choice. So, even though you won't owe any taxes when you withdraw this money, you won't be able to lower your current taxable income.

You can look for the best investments for your needs with the aid of a wealth mindset. Who wouldn't want to earn money while they sleep, after all?

3. Never stop working hard
The mindset of the millionaire wealthy includes hustling.
It's time to invest in what matters most now that you have a solid foundation for growing your money:

Yourself.

Reduce time-wasting activities like watching television or scrolling through social media if you want to promote a wealth mindset. Over two hours are daily spent on social media platforms worldwide.

Take care of your body rather than scrolling aimlessly. If you aren't already paying attention to your physical and mental health, start by learning and putting into practice "better health habits" like eating well, getting enough sleep, and exercising in the right way.

Another suggestion is to work on your negotiating abilities. When it comes to negotiating contracts with clients, salaries, or bills, affluent individuals always win and can get more money for themselves.

By starting a side business, you can make extra money. 44 million Americans have a side business where they make an average of $25 per hour, whether it be driving for a ride-sharing company, online teaching, or even officiating weddings.

You won't even feel like you're working if you find a niche you're enthusiastic about.
Acquire new talents in fields that interest you as well. You never know when a skill you pick up today will open up a door for you tomorrow.

4. Keep a positive outlook
woman grinning to emphasize the value of having a prosperous and cheerful mindset

You may be familiar with the "law of attraction."

According to the law of attraction, opposites attract. In other words, comparable thoughts and behaviors are attracted to our own.

Positive things will occur if you think positively.

If you consider how to acquire wealth, you will increase the amount of wealth in your life.

You must encourage optimistic ideas of prosperity and abundance. You'll become disheartened and give up on your goals if you focus on the bad.

Start by clearing your mind of all bad thoughts. In their stead, consider the following:

"I'll be wealthy,"
I am competent enough.
I can succeed.
The path to prosperity is difficult, but if you start putting obstacles in your way, it won't get

any simpler. You must be certain that you will succeed.

What Is The Time Frame For Developing A Wealth Mindset?
The wonderful thing about creating a wealth mindset is that you can get started right away with education, planning, and action.

Start small and focus on manageable objectives first. These little investments grow over time, much like compound interest, and help you get closer to your financial objectives.

Your wealth ambitions will be on the fast track to achievement in a matter of months, weeks, or even days.

There is no easy recipe to follow to become wealthy. Perhaps you'll come up with a wonderful concept and follow it through. Perhaps you'll find a fantastic co-founder for your business. You might put in a lot of effort, like the majority of us, but you'll also make wise financial decisions and invest your way to wealth.

Everyone must ultimately choose the path that is best for them.

But, those who can cultivate and maintain a wealth mindset will prevail in the end.

Identifying And Overcoming Limiting Beliefs About Money

How to Cure Your Money-Related Limiting Beliefs

Do you think your money-related limiting beliefs are preventing you from enjoying the financial plenty you desire? You are in the proper location. Here, you'll discover how your limiting money beliefs have manifested in your life and how to start eradicating them so that your financial situation can start to improve.

We are all aware of the value of money. Possessing money provides security, opens the door to novel experiences, aids in problem-solving, provides access to healthcare, etc.

Your quality of life may be much reduced and your level of stress may increase if you don't have enough money. Several things are off-limits to you, and you might not be able to have all of your needs addressed.

Although there are severe problems with all of those things, it is simple to blame a lack of money on the government, society, or the wealthy, and we have all heard success stories of people who come from less privileged homes than our own.

What do they possess that you lack? It's not a matter of luck or unique abilities that you could never expect to possess. Their worldview and financial outlook are empowering rather than constricting.

If you are aware that your relationship with money is negative because it only brings you to worry and pain, this lack of attitude is the product of the beliefs you've developed in the past.

What Are the Roots of Limiting Beliefs About Money?

The root of a lack of attitude is fear. It doesn't matter if you're afraid of running out of money, of having it taken away from you, or of being unable to handle it because you don't believe in yourself.

With very few exceptions, most of us have either personally struggled with money or had a family history of doing so.

Or perhaps you didn't have financial difficulties as a child, but you went through something else that made you believe you weren't deserving of wealth, security, or success.

You may have grown up witnessing your parents argue over money, which may have made you feel insecure and led you to link money with danger. Maybe you heard "we can't afford that" every time you went into the store to buy something.

Maybe the grownups in your household would whine about greedy rich people or the government stealing their money.

You learned from this that not everyone has access to the same amount of money, that someone will always steal it from you, and that some people are deserving of it while others are not. It implanted restrictive money notions in your subconscious mind, and you act on them without being cognizant of them or knowing why you behave as you do.

How Your Finances Are Managed by Your Subconscious Mind

Our subconscious minds function like a piggy bank when we are young. Every single thing we hear and experience causes us to form a belief about how the world functions and our subconscious mind then store those ideas.

Then, as we mature, we begin to make our own decisions and engage in social interactions with people in the outside world. We begin taking money out of our subconscious belief system (our piggy bank) in the shape of our decisions.

The conscious mind makes those decisions in reaction to what it observes in the outside environment. The conscious mind tries to use logic when it processes what we see and hears to help us make the best decision, but it is strongly influenced by those ingrained ideas we developed as children when we weren't able to use logic to make sense of our experiences.

how the mind's subconscious creates stifling money beliefs

So, our belief system serves as a filter for every decision we make. Although the cognitive part of you recognizes the advantages of earning more money each month, your subconscious beliefs tell you that it won't happen. It challenges your conscious desires without your knowledge since money is a limited resource and we are only permitted a certain amount.

The subconscious mind can make decisions up to 10 seconds before we're even aware of them, contrary to what we commonly believe (the conscious mind is the part of you that is aware and thinking right now).

We make 95% of our decisions subconsciously, therefore if you have a lot of limiting money beliefs bouncing around in your head, they are manifesting in your life daily.

Symptoms of a Poor Mentality
How do you know that those ingrained assumptions have caused you to adopt a mindset of scarcity? These indications:

When you spend money, you experience fear, remorse, or shame (even when you do have enough money).
You are caught in a cycle of abundance and scarcity. For a while, money emerges, and then it vanishes in an instant. You never move forward because the pattern keeps repeating.
You think that having money is a finite resource, and there is a cap on how much you can have at any given time.
You think the only way to have money is to be miserable and labor yourself to death.
You're positive there will never be a way for you to earn extra money.

When you see someone having something you want, you feel envious and resentful.

You fear that a costly emergency may arise and deplete your savings, or that you won't be able to pay for it at all.

You fall into never-work get-rich-quick scams. Perhaps you have lost money as a result of your uncle's dubious business plan even though you intuitively knew you shouldn't have given him a cent. Or you lost a ton of money by falling for an MLM scam.

Instead of purchasing something because you enjoy, want, or need them, you do it because they are inexpensive or "just in case."

Because "the man" would take more in taxes, you're terrified of earning more money.

You don't establish lofty financial objectives because you don't believe you can accomplish them.

Because giving things away would cost money, you keep junk you don't want around.

You never spend money on pleasurable things and save every penny.

You don't do anything to improve your finances since you don't think they will ever get better.

To fit in or impress someone, you spend money you know you shouldn't and get up in debt.

You find the idea of sharing your money offensive (wealthy individuals can also have a lack of attitude; just consider all the billionaires who refuse to pay their staff a living salary).
You avoid checking your bank account and keeping track of your spending because you find it stressful.
Even when you can, your initial thought is always, "I can't afford that," whenever you see anything you desire.

How to Cure Your Limiting Beliefs About Money
The good news is that we can rewire our limiting money beliefs, even if you currently feel a little overwhelmed. Both our views and our brains are not immutable.

Because of neuroplasticity, we can create new neural networks in our brains. As a result, you can change your reaction to seeing a bill from being stressed to feeling sure that you'll always have enough money to cover any expenses that arise.

The steps to overcome a lack of mindset are shown below.

how to overcome your limiting financial beliefs
1. Determine Your Money-Related Limiting Beliefs
Consider any unpleasant connotations you may have with money, whether they stem from personal encounters or the prism through which society views money.

Write down your inquiries and your responses:

How does looking at my bank account make me feel?
What do I think when I see an expensive item that I want?
What do I fear will occur if I genuinely succeed and get rich?
What financial lessons did my parents or other early educators impart to me?
How have things been with me and money? What recurring pattern is this?

Do I refrain from contemplating or gazing at money?

Would I know how to handle money if I won the lottery? Would I believe I deserved it?

How do I discuss money? Do I frequently utter phrases like "I'll be broke forever" or "wealthy people are evil"?

You must dig deep and be prepared to be incredibly open-minded and vulnerable. Don't feel guilty about your money views when you contemplate; do it with self-love.

2. Modify your viewpoint on wealth

You need to alter your attitude after identifying some limiting assumptions you hold regarding money.

What would be the polar opposite of your limiting money beliefs? What values would a successful person hold?

How would someone who was significantly more powerful and affluent than you in an alternate scenario approach money? Write down how the person thinks about money after getting into that mindset.

Examine your language when referring to wealthy individuals to see if you might adopt a fresh perspective. Here are a few illustrations.

If you've ever regarded someone as wealthy and believed that their wealth caused them to be selfish or evil, recognize that they were already those things, whether or not they had money. Even if they lose everything, they will still be greedy or wicked; the problem is not the money, it's them.

What if there were more wealthy decent individuals who made the world a better place? What if you were one of those people who used their money to improve the world? Decide that you can live in that world in your imagination.

Do you save cash out of anticipation of a catastrophe? That can cause you to unconsciously look for them. Spend money wisely and not out of fear of running out of money. Saving money feels nice.

Instead of an emergency or rainy day fund, I refer to my savings account as my Feel Good Fund. Not because of any fear that something horrible may occur, but rather because it seems like a high score in a game, I enjoy seeing a large number in my savings account.

And it feels incredibly wonderful to know that I can use that money in the future to buy something special.

Simply examine your assumptions and consider how you may perceive something otherwise.

The solution might not appear immediately away, so revisit your limiting ideas later to examine them objectively.

It can be simpler to say than to do to reprogram beliefs. Sometimes all it takes to get rid of a very dumb belief is acknowledging you have one, but other times it requires more effort.

3. Engage in Abundance Mindset Practice
How do you already have plenty?

Your initial response could be, "Ma'am, I am NOT plentiful at this time!

"And hey, maybe your bank account is negative and you have a backlog of bills, that's okay.

But there are other forms of abundance besides money.

Possessing a wonderful shoe collection, being surrounded by nature, having a functioning car, having a roof over your head, and having food in the refrigerator are all examples of abundance.

Being plentiful is more than just having a specific amount in your income or bank account.

Money is still important because we need it to survive and experience certain things in life, but taking the time to recognize all the other forms of plenty helps us develop the correct mindset. And you'll value it even more when the money you want does come in.

Also, because your brain will search for more of the things that are significant to you, it teaches your subconscious mind to seek out additional opportunities to get positive things.

4. Be persistent and strive to keep an abundance mindset.
It doesn't necessarily mean that the money starts flowing in right away just because you start altering your perspective on money and destroying those outdated, restricting money ideas.

Remember that having wealth is not prohibited by any written rule in the sky. You are just as worthy and deserving of any amount of money you desire as everyone else.

Maintain your efforts to change the way you have been thinking about money. It won't immediately become ingrained in your brain, but with time and repetition, your belief system will begin to shift. After that, you'll begin to act naturally to build that money.

Finding ways to raise your income might take time, and it's normal to feel impatient and upset when the money doesn't appear. Just keep working on yourself, not just because you desire money but also because you want to be liberated from those constraints.

The day a seed is planted does not necessarily result in fruit bearing. When nothing seems to be happening, don't give up hope.

5. Seek for Possibilities to Generate and Acquire Money
You will start to discover ways to create money without even thinking about it if you alter your belief system and form empowering attitudes about money.

You blocked off opportunities to make money because of your outdated, restricting money views. They were there, but because your beliefs function as a filter that distorts reality, you were unable to notice them or take action on them (as you perceive them).

In 2018, for instance, my intuition said, "Hey Katrina, you should start a blog," but my limiting beliefs countered, "No way, you don't have anything useful to share with the world and it won't make any money." As a result, I didn't establish a blog that year, but I continued to work on my beliefs on the inside. A year later, when my intuition again prompted me to start a blog, I was able to have faith in my abilities and launch A Point of Light.

While doing the inner work did not yield immediate benefits, they did develop with time, and finally, I was able to recognize the chances I had previously missed and act on them.

Be willing to think outside the box as you strive to change your money beliefs. Be prepared to experience discomfort.

Gently correct your previous beliefs as they appear and remark, "That's not possible for me." You may make "I'm ready to receive wealth in new and unexpected ways" your mantra.

Be open to receiving money in ways you previously didn't think you could. Accept the opportunities you previously declined.

Continue your work and be prepared to take action when your intuition signals that this is the right course of action. Let's leave.

CHAPTER 2:

CREATING A BUDGET AND MANAGING YOUR EXPENSES

You can better track your spending if you have a budget. You can create a strategy to achieve your financial objectives as well as set aside money for bills and other needs.

To begin, adhere to these guidelines. As the timeline for your budget, use how frequently you get paid. For instance, create a weekly budget if you get paid weekly.

1. Log your earnings.
Keep track of when and how much money is coming in. Calculate an average sum if you don't have a steady income.

Create a list of every dollar that comes in, including:

the amount

from where

how frequently (weekly, fortnightly, monthly, or yearly)

This money may come from your salary, retirement benefits, government payments or benefits, or income from investments.

2. tally up your spending

Your regular expenses are your "needs"—the things you really must have to survive. They consist of:

For instance, fixed expenses

mortgage or rent payments
telephone, gas, and electricity bills
municipal fees
home costs, such as groceries and food
healthcare expenses and insurance
transportation expenses, such as vehicle registration or bus fares
family expenses, such as those for infant supplies, daycare, tuition, and extracurricular activities
Debt costs, for instance:

payments on personal loans
payment with a credit card
home loan payments
Unexpected costs, for instance:

auto services and repairs
medical expenses
added school expenses
pet prices
Examine your bills or bank statements to confirm that you have listed all of your spendings. Specify the purpose, cost, and date of the expense.

Use your list of transactions if you kept track of your spending.

3. Establish a spending cap.
You can spend and save the money that remains after expenses.

Your disposable income is used on "wants" like entertainment, dining out, and hobbies.

Create a plan for how you wish to use your discretionary income. This will make it easier for you to track where it goes and stay under your budget.

4. Establish a savings objective.
You can use your budget to help you achieve a savings goal.

You may determine how much of it you'd like to save after you know how much money you have for "wants."

Savings might serve as a safety net for unforeseen costs. Regularly setting aside even a small sum will have an impact.

5. Adapt your spending plan
It's crucial to modify your budget when circumstances change so that it fits your demands and your way of life.

For instance, if your costs start to rise, you might need to cut back on your spending or alter your savings objective. If you receive a pay raise or pay off some debt, you might also be able to increase your savings.

Use Excel budget spreadsheet to create and save your budget online.

6. Facilitate budgeting
Consider opening different bank accounts to make budgeting simpler. You might've:

a transaction account used for costs and bills
a spending account for transactions
a savings account paying greater interest
Then, by establishing a recurring transfer to your savings account every payday, you may automate your budget. Also, you can program direct debits for when your bills are due.

Why setting a budget is crucial for accumulating wealth

Many people spend far more than they make, which causes them to gradually accumulate debt before they even realize it. Budgeting is useful in this situation.
Budgeting: What Is It?
Simply explained, budgeting is making a plan for your financial spending. This enables you to

estimate the amount of time you have to do the tasks you need to or want to do. Prioritizing your demands based on their importance might also be helpful.

What is budgeting, and why do you need one? Why Is A Budget Necessary?

1. A budget may help you forecast your spending and establish plans for long-term aims like purchasing an investment, starting your own business, or making a down payment on a home, as well as short-term ones like even taking a vacation.

2. You spend what you have - One area where people have always overspent their means is in discretionary spending. This particular requirement is met by following a specified budget and using saved funds. This will undoubtedly help you avoid debt or, if you already have it, work your way out of it.

3. makes you happy when you retire - It's crucial to allocate a portion of your budget to investing. Later in life, this will become evident.

4. Emergencies - Everyone experiences life's ups and downs, and you never know when the unexpected will strike. This is why it's so important to set aside money for emergencies. Knowing you have money on hand "just in case" gives you comfort.

5. Reduce wasteful spending - Making a budget may assist you to realize which expenses you are making too much money on. You'll begin debating the crucial issue of whether or not anything is required. Your spending habits will undoubtedly change as a result, and you'll be better able to focus on your future financial goals and ambitions.

Strategies for creating a budget that works for you
.
For workers in many different occupations, budgeting is a crucial personal and professional skill. It enables you to support a company's expansion and aids in ensuring financial stability. You may better manage your funds

and develop your financial skills to advance in your job by learning smart budgeting tactics.

In this book, we define a budget plan, provide examples of budget strategies, and offer budget maintenance advice.

What exactly is a budget plan?
A formal method of managing a group of funds is a budget strategy. To make sure their spending doesn't outpace their income, many people adopt budgeting techniques in their daily lives. Others utilize budgeting techniques to assist in achieving financial objectives like buying a new automobile or setting aside a specific sum of money for retirement. Many experts also employ budgeting techniques at work to guarantee that a division or business can cover all costs and maybe invest in new prospects.

Budget-friendly tactics to try
To find the one that best fits your goals and circumstances, you can experiment with a variety of budgeting techniques. Here are 12

practical budgeting techniques you may utilize to accomplish your financial goals:

1. subtractive spending

One of the simplest types of budgeting is subtraction budgeting. Using this approach, you add up all of your monthly expenses and take the result from your total monthly income. You can save and enjoy yourself with the money you have left over.

2. Cash management

When you stick to a cash budget, also known as an envelope budget, you pay for things with actual cash rather than managing digital currency. Having cash on hand can frequently make tracking money easier for people who have problems seeing their money in digital form.

In a cash budgeting strategy, you cash your paycheck and use the actual notes and coins to pay for your expenses rather than depositing them into your bank account. Some people seal the exact amount of money they need for bills like rent and utilities until they are paid to prevent wasting it on other things.

3. Using a proportional budget

You divide all of your spendings into three areas with a proportionate budgeting strategy: savings, needs, and wants. The amount of your money that you wish to allocate to each of these categories is then decided upon. After that, you can allocate your money among those groups as necessary.

4. Budgeting with two banks

When budgeting with two banks, you pay yourself before you pay any other bills. This enables you to fund any savings plans and make whatever purchases you wish. Opening a checking account into which you deposit your paycheck is one practical use of this concept. Then, make arrangements for an automatic transfer from that account to a different one, leaving a modest sum of your paycheck in the first account. You can then use the funds in your secondary account to support yourself while keeping the monies in your primary account set aside for future purchases or unexpected expenses.

5. Budgeting automatically

You can take use of the built-in budgeting solutions that banks offer by using automatic budgeting. Consider setting up automatic transfers and bill payments. This guarantees that you fulfill your savings objectives and pay all of your bills on time without having to make any actual payments or deposits.

6. Budgeting using a website or app

Several tools are available to help you keep track of your spending and efficiently develop a custom budget that suits your needs and goals. Software programs called budget applications sync with your bank accounts and compile all of your information in one location so you always know how much money you have coming in and going out. Think about utilizing one of these applications to assist you in creating a special budgeting system tailored to your needs and your spending habits.

7. With a 50/30/20 budget

The 50/30/20 approach is a well-known budgeting technique that makes use of ratios to aid with money management. Fundamentally, with this plan, 50% of your income is allocated to your needs, or non-negotiable necessities, such as rent and utilities, 30% is allocated to your wants, or personal expenses, such as entertainment and dining out, and 20% is allocated to savings and debt repayment. The 50/30/20 budgeting method might help those who desire to purchase a home or start an emergency savings account.

8. Budgeting for multiple accounts

A digital adaptation of the cash envelope budgeting method is the multi-accounting budgeting system. By using this method, you create numerous bank accounts, each of which is assigned a particular spending or saving objective. To ensure that you pay your bills on time, you can utilize automatic bill pay services and transfers to automatically send the right amount of money to each account.

9. Budgeting from nothing

Another conventional technique that emphasizes making sure you have enough money set aside to pay for your basic needs is the zero-based budgeting approach. With this approach, you deduct monthly expenses from your income until you have a balance that fully covers your monthly priorities. To achieve zero waste with your resources, you must make sure to account for all of your money.

10. Budgeting for emergencies and saving

A savings and emergency planning technique could be quite useful for maximizing your savings. With this strategy, a specified portion of your salary is placed into a general savings account that may be used to fund specific purchases, like a home or a vehicle. A further portion goes into an emergency fund for unforeseen costs like auto repairs or job loss.

11. Budgeting with prepaid debit cards

Prepaid debit cards are an effective budgeting tool for people who loathe carrying cash but find it difficult to control their credit card usage. It works as a hybrid of the cash envelope system and the multiple-account budgeting technique, except for daily expenses, instead of using cash or a card tied to your bank account, it uses prepaid debit cards. By doing this, you can prevent overdrawing your account and making unwise purchases.

12. Prioritize spending

Setting your priorities rather than relying on the established priorities of others is part of creating a priority budget. You make a list of every expense you have and your top spending priorities, then you rank them according to importance. The amount of money you want to allocate to each category can then be decided.

Advice for staying within your budget

A great first step in effectively saving money is deciding on a budget plan. You may achieve your short- and long-term budgeting objectives by making sure you adhere to the rules you outlined in your budget. Here are some pointers to help you stick to your spending plan:

Monitor your spending. Tracking your expenditure and identifying areas where you can make adjustments to meet your short- and long-term financial objectives is one of the greatest methods to make the most of your budget.

Review and revision. Review your budget frequently to make sure you are staying within your spending restrictions. Your budget should be updated and modified as necessary to account for shifting goals and spending patterns.

Set objectives. Make sure the objectives you establish for your budget are manageable and achievable. To assist you in setting practical financial objectives, think about adopting the SMART goals method.

Apply tools. To help you gain a clear understanding of your spending and saving, use tools like apps and online money monitors.

Remain inspired. Look at your long-term goals frequently to help you remember why you're using a budget and to keep yourself inspired to save.

Use credit cards less often. With a credit card, it is possible to easily overspend. If you frequently rack up unneeded credit card debt, think about switching to cash or debit cards to prevent overspending.

Tips for reducing expenses and increasing savings

It makes sense to consider acquiring a better job or starting a side business if, like many Americans, you frequently find yourself with extra money at the end of the month. Nothing wrong with that, to be sure. Yet, your income may not be the true issue; rather, it may be your spending. You might need to substantially cut back on spending.

How do you go about that? There are numerous strategies to reduce costs and make savings. Just be aware of where to look.

1. Monitor Your Spending Patterns

If you've ever had a child in your home, you are aware of how easily they can vanish if you aren't paying close attention to them. Well, money works similarly. Maintain a written record of your expenditures. This is a straightforward answer, but it requires discipline. It's practically impossible to determine where to minimize costs if you don't know where your money is going.

To be clear, everything is included, including the $1 you spent on a soft drink. Just the act of doing this will cause you to question if you need to incur that expense. Utilize a journal, spreadsheet, or financial app. You'll have the data you need for the following stage of the procedure if you do this for at least one month, preferably two.

Make the most of your money at the grocery store.
Couponing can be a simple and enjoyable way to reduce your monthly shopping expenditure.

2. Establish a Budget
At its most basic, setting a budget needs three steps: knowing your income, knowing your expenses, and planning to spend less than your income so you can save the difference. The benefit of budgeting is that you may prioritize your spending to reach your objectives if you are aware of your income and costs.

Although it's a good idea to keep detailed financial records, not everyone should use that approach. The 50-30-20 rule is an alternative strategy. Set aside 50% of your income for necessities (such as a place to live, utilities, insurance, food, clothing, taxes, and debt repayments), 30% for wants (such as eating out, entertainment, and luxury), and 20% for savings.

You'll need self-control to refrain from spending the money set aside for savings. Yet, if you carefully consider ways to reduce costs, you can do it.

3. Subscriptions for Updates
Here's a simple question: Are there any publications, streaming services, or subscriptions that you don't use frequently or at all? Reject them. Have you utilized this good or service in the past several months? Can you locate a less expensive model? Eliminate it. When money isn't as tight, you can always re-subscribe if you find out you missed it.

You should stop receiving any email newsletters or product catalogs that encourage you to make impulsive purchases, even when they aren't directly costing you money. You can sign up again later, but for now, you must deal with the situation at hand.

4. Reduce Your Electricity Bills
Power and water are necessities, but there are ways to reduce your utility costs.

Replace burned-out incandescent light bulbs with LEDs. They are more expensive to purchase but more than pay for themselves because they last longer and use less electricity. Instead of using wattage, which measures the amount of electricity used, to determine the proper bulb, utilize the lumens number, which represents the quantity of light output.

For your heating and cooling system, install a programmable thermostat. You can reduce your utility costs by adjusting the temperature of your home when you're not there. Just before you get home from work, you can set it to restore to a more comfortable temperature.

Plug in all unneeded electrical equipment. When not in use, a lot of electronic devices utilize a tiny amount of electricity, which adds up. Using power strips or timers to turn devices on and off is another option to reduce electricity usage. Power can be controlled by "smart" power strips so that DVD players only receive power while the TV is on.

Your water heater's temperature should be decreased. It wastes energy to keep it hotter because you probably don't need it to be any hotter than 130 degrees Fahrenheit. Energy can be saved by insulating hot water pipes and using a water heater blanket.

Your home's leaks should be sealed. Air leaky doors and windows should be caulked and weather-stripped. Fix any air leaks where electrical wiring, ducting, or piping enters walls, floors, or ceilings. Put foam gaskets underneath the wall-mounted switch and outlet plates.

As you leave a room, turn off the lights.
Fix leaky faucets and toilets. Shower for fewer minutes. When purchasing a new dishwasher or

washing machine, look for the Energy Star label to help you conserve water.

5. Alternatives for Cheaper Housing

Any effort to save money must take housing into account because it is a significant expense. Although owning a home is ingrained in the American mentality as the ideal way to live, it is important to consider whether this is the case for you, or at least at this particular moment. Renting has several benefits, including affordability. Rent can be less expensive per month than a mortgage because you don't have to pay for repairs, upfront financing fees for a mortgage, or homeowner association dues.

If you already rent, moving to a less costly neighborhood or into a smaller rental home or apartment may allow you to reduce your monthly payments. A popular alternative is to get a roommate. Getting a roommate lowers your monthly expenses because the rent for a two-bedroom apartment is not twice as much as a one-bedroom. Negotiate your lease renewal when the time comes. Because they lose money when your apartment is vacant if you move out, landlords prefer to have dependable tenants.

There are, of course, many benefits to owning a home. But, there are ways to guarantee a cheaper mortgage payment if you want to purchase a home. Prices for real estate could be lower if you're ready to drive a few miles further. You can avoid paying for private mortgage insurance if you put down at least 20% of the purchase price. Refinancing may result in a lower monthly payment if mortgage interest rates have significantly down since you purchased your house.

6. Debt consolidation

Debt is probably a significant portion of your monthly expenses unless you pay cash for everything, a great goal that few people attain. Credit card debt, auto loans, and student loan debt all pile up. Each of those debts requires a different outlay, and each one might have represented the best bargain you could have gotten at the time. But perhaps you might improve by treating your debt as a single entity.

Several debts are combined into a single monthly payment through debt consolidation. If you have a balance on one or more high-interest credit cards or student loans, it may be very helpful. As long as you make your monthly payments on time, a single loan with a lower interest rate can cut your monthly expenses and pay off your obligations more quickly. It might also be beneficial to combine your credit cards into one low-interest card, but you might only have 18 months to pay off your obligations during the promotional period before interest rates rise.

A debt management plan, which you can get through a nonprofit credit counseling program, is another alternative for dealing with credit card debt. To pay off their credit card debt, individuals can use credit counseling services' assistance in creating an acceptable monthly budget. Card issuers offer to cut their interest rates in exchange for a single monthly payment from customers, which the nonprofit counseling organization then distributes to each card issuer.

7. Compare prices for insurance

How diligently did you look for the lowest prices on homeowners' and auto insurance when you purchased your home or vehicle? not at all? There is no better time than the present to compare prices. There are many insurance providers, therefore you might find that getting your auto and home insurance from the same provider or other providers will result in cost savings. Most insurance providers provide a discount for combining.

Increasing your deductible—the amount you must pay before insurance pays a claim—can lower your vehicle insurance monthly costs. For those who rarely seek medical attention and simply want to make sure they're protected in case of an emergency, there are high-deductible health insurance plans that also come with reduced premiums. Term life insurance, which expires after a predetermined amount of time, has cheaper monthly rates than whole life insurance, which provides coverage for the rest of your life. One option for term insurance is to have it expire when you retire and your family is no longer dependent on your income.

8. At-Home Meals

You must eat. Yet dining out is not required. We understand that eating out or ordering takeout is more convenient and perhaps more delicious than food prepared in your house. That costs a lot more money, though. A lot. You don't have to follow a strict "rice and beans, beans and rice" diet to have a significant impact on your financial situation. Yet you must make reductions.

Lack of self-assurance in the kitchen. For beginners, there are countless cookbooks and YouTube videos available. Prepare a large number of your favorite foods and freeze the leftovers for later use. Purchase nonperishable goods. Utilize coupons for food. Instead of recognizable brands, choose generic or store brands for canned products. Spending less on coffee purchases can also help you save money.

9. Shop With a List

Fantastic if you're purchasing your food from a grocery store rather than a restaurant! Making a shopping list in advance and sticking to it is a tried-and-true technique to reduce the amount of money you spend at the grocery store. Avoid the urge to make an impulsive purchase when you arrive at the store. It will be best if you structure your list around any sales that the store has publicized.

10. Your Credit Cards Being Frozen
Credit cards have many benefits, but one of those benefits is that they are quite convenient. It's so simple to buy something you shouldn't, but you decide you'll pay for it when your credit card bill arrives. Many people incur credit card debt in this way. Additionally, even if you keep your credit card balance at zero, money spent on impulsive purchases takes away from funds that may be used for more crucial purchases.

Therefore try to find a less convenient way to use your credit card. Your wallet or purse should be left at home. You might think about literally freezing your credit cards in a block of ice, which may sound ridiculous. Although it will take some time for them to thaw out, you will still have them if necessary. At that time, you may decide to reevaluate if making that purchase is actually in your best interests. (This is different from freezing your credit to prevent identity theft, which can be a good action but may not help you reduce spending.)

11. Switch to Cash Only

If you're serious about dramatically reducing your expenditure, commit to just using cash going forward, if not permanently. This makes you accountable for every dollar you spend, and research shows that people are more frugal with cash than with credit cards. You can't live above your means if you use cash.

Your regular, necessary bills, such as your rent or mortgage, utilities, and the like, are paid through automatic withdrawals to make this easier. You can only spend the remaining money that you have.

12. Clear your debts

You should pay off your debt if you want to cut costs and save money. This is particularly true with credit card debt, which often has an interest rate that is significantly greater than that of traditional loans. If you pay interest, you won't have any money left over for other things you might need or want. By doing so, you are compensating for the ease of obtaining something before you could afford it. The cost of the purchase increases with the length of time it takes to pay it off.

Depending on how much debt you have, there are a variety of debt repayment alternatives. Although debt consolidation may assist, you still need to commit to paying it off completely. List all of your debts and rank them from highest to lowest interest rate if you are unable to refinance. Pay off the debt with the highest interest rate next, followed by the next highest, and so on. Including paying off debt in your monthly budget. Decide when you want to be debt-free and take the necessary steps to achieve it.

Start today by reducing your expenses.
Stop waiting. Don't think twice. Don't think and reflect. Start now. The more you save, the faster you start and finish. Consider visiting with a credit counselor at a nonprofit credit counseling organization like InCharge Debt Solutions if

your obligations are so substantial that you are uncertain about your capacity to pay them off.

CHAPTER 3:

INVESTING IN YOUR FUTURE

When you first start, especially during periods of inflation when your paycheck can only buy a fraction of what it used to, things like bread, gas, and a house, it may seem as though all you can afford are rent, utilities, debt payments, and groceries. But once you've figured out how to budget for those regular costs (and save at least some money for an emergency fund), it's time to start investing. Choosing what to invest in and how much to invest in is the challenging part.

You'll have many questions as you learn more about investing, not the least of which is: What are the best investment strategies for beginners?, how much money do I need, and how do I get started? Our tour guide will respond to these queries and others.

To start investing this year, follow these five steps:

1. Start your investments as soon as you can.
One of the best ways to get good returns on your money is to invest when you're young. Thanks to compound earnings, your investment returns now begin to generate their return. Your account balance can accumulate over time thanks to compounding.

At the same time, a lot of people ponder whether they can start with not much cash. Simply put: Yes.

Due to low or no investment minimums, zero commissions, and fractional shares, investing with smaller sums of money is now easier than ever. Numerous investments, including mutual funds, exchange-traded funds, and index funds, are readily available for relatively small sums.

If you're worried that your contribution won't be enough, concentrate on what feels manageable in light of your goals and financial situation. "Make a regular contribution to your investments, whether it's $50 per month or $5,000 per month,"

How that functions in real life: Assume you invest $200 each month for ten years and generate an average annual return of 6%. You'll have $33,300 after the ten years is over. You have made contributions totaling $24,200 of that sum ($200 per month), and you have earned interest totaling $9,100 on your investment.

Investing early gives you decades to ride out the market's ups and downs as well as decades for your money to grow. Of course, there will be ups and downs in the stock market. Start right away, even if you have to do so slowly.

Use our inflation calculator to see how inflation can reduce your savings if you don't invest if you're still not convinced of the value of investing.

2. Determine the amount to invest.
Your financial situation, your investment goal, and the deadline for achieving it all will determine how much you should invest.

Retirement is a typical investment objective. As a general rule, you should aim to invest 10% to 15% of your annual income toward retirement. That probably sounds impossible right now, but you can begin small and gradually work your way up to it. (Use our retirement calculator to determine a more precise retirement goal.)

Your first investing milestone is simple if your employer offers matching funds for retirement accounts like 401(k)s: just make at least the minimum contribution to the account to qualify for the full match. You don't want to miss out on that free money, especially since your employer matches counts toward that objective.

Consider your time horizon and the amount you require for other investing goals, such as home ownership, travel, or education, then work backward to divide that amount into monthly or weekly investments.

3. Open a brokerage account.
You can invest for retirement in an individual retirement account (IRA), such as a traditional or Roth IRA, if you're one of the many people

who don't have access to an employer-sponsored retirement account like a 401(k).

Retirement accounts, which are intended to be used for retirement and have limitations on when and how you can withdraw your money, should be avoided if you're investing for another goal.

Instead, think about opening a taxable brokerage account that allows withdrawals at any time with no additional tax or penalty. If you want to keep investing after you've reached the maximum limit for your IRA retirement contributions, brokerage accounts are another great choice (as the contribution limits are often significantly lower for IRAs than employer-sponsored retirement accounts).

4. Select a financial strategy.
Your investment strategy is based on the amount of money you need to save to reach your goals, as well as your time frame.

Almost all of your savings can be invested in stocks if your goal is something like retirement, which is more than 20 years away. However, selecting individual stocks can be difficult and time-consuming. For this reason, for the majority of investors, the best way to invest in stocks is through inexpensive stock mutual funds, index funds, or ETFs.

The risk associated with stocks makes it better to keep your money safe in an online savings account, cash management account, or low-risk investment portfolio if you're saving for a short-term goal and will need the money in less than five years. Here, we list the top choices for making quick savings.

You can open an investment account (including an IRA) through a robo-advisor, an investment management service that builds and manages your investment portfolio using computer algorithms if you are unable or unwilling to make a decision.

Low-cost ETFs and index funds make up a large portion of the portfolios created by robo-advisors. Robots allow you to get started quickly because they have low costs and low or no minimums. For portfolio management, they demand a small fee of typically 0.25 percent of your account balance.

5. Know your investing alternatives
You must choose what to invest in after deciding how to do so. Every investment involves some level of risk, so it's critical to comprehend each one, its level of risk, and whether or not it aligns with your goals. For those who are just starting, the most common investments include:

Stocks
A stock is a unit of ownership in one particular business. Equities are another name for stocks.

Stocks are bought for a share price, which, depending on the company, can range from a few dollars to several thousand. We advise buying stocks through mutual funds, which we'll go into more depth about below.

Bonds

A bond is effectively a loan to a business or government agency that promises to repay you over a specified time. You receive interest in the interim.

Generally speaking, bonds are less risky than stocks since you know exactly when and how much you will be paid back. Bonds should, however, only make up a modest portion of a long-term investing portfolio because of their poor long-term returns.

A mutual fund
A mutual fund is a collection of investments that have been bundled. Investors can buy a variety of stocks and bonds in one transaction through mutual funds, saving them the time and effort of selecting individual securities. Mutual funds are inherently more diversified than individual equities, making them generally less risky.

While some mutual funds are professionally managed, index funds, a subset of mutual funds, track the performance of a particular stock market index, such as the S&P 500. Index funds can charge cheaper fees than actively managed mutual funds because they do not require expert management.

Without a minimum investment requirement, most 401(k) programs offer a carefully selected range of mutual or index funds; nevertheless, outside of those plans, these funds may demand a minimum of $1,000 or more.

Traded-based funds
An ETF has numerous separate investments that are grouped, similar to a mutual fund. The distinction is that ETFs are bought at a share price and traded throughout the day like stocks.

ETFs are an excellent choice for novice investors or individuals with tight budgets because the share price of an ETF is frequently lower than the minimum investment requirement of a mutual fund. ETFs can also be index funds.

Understanding different types of investments

Investing: What Is It?

In general, investing is putting money to work over a while in a project or endeavor in the hopes of generating profits (i.e., profits that exceed the amount of the initial investment). It's the act of allocating resources, typically capital (i.e., money), with the hope of making money, making gains, or making a profit.

One can engage in a variety of activities (directly or indirectly), such as utilizing capital to launch a business or buying assets like real estate to rent it out and/or sell it at a profit in the future.

In a contrast to saving, investing involves putting money to work, which carries an implied risk that the connected project(s) could fail and cause a financial loss. The other way that investing differs from speculation is that the latter involves wagering on short-term price swings rather than putting the money to work.

Investing entails allocating capital (cash) to ventures or pursuits anticipated to produce a profit over the long term.

The sort of returns produced varies on the project or asset; real estate can result in both rent and capital gains; many stocks pay dividends quarterly; bonds often pay interest regularly.

Risk and return are essentially the two sides of the same investing coin; minimal risk typically translates into low predicted profits, while larger returns are typically accompanied by higher risk.

Investors have two options: they either handle their own money themselves or hire a professional money manager.

The level of risk involved, the length of the holding period, and the source of rewards determine whether purchasing security falls under the category of investing or speculating.

Knowing about Investment

A person invests to increase their money over time. The fundamental tenet of investing is the expectation of a favorable return in the form of income or price appreciation with statistical significance. There is a fairly broad range of assets in which one can invest and generate a return.

In investment, risk and return are inversely correlated; low risk typically translates into low predicted returns, whereas larger profits are typically associated with increased risk. Basic investments like Certificates of Deposit (CDs) are at the low end of the risk spectrum; bonds or fixed-income instruments are at the higher end, and stocks or equities are seen as riskier. Generally speaking, commodities and derivatives are among the riskiest assets. Besides investing in tangible assets like real estate or land, one can also do so in delicate things like fine art and antiques.

Within the same asset class, risk and return expectations can differ significantly. A micro-cap that trades on a tiny exchange will have a substantially different risk-return profile than a blue chip that trades on the New York Stock Exchange.

Depending on the type of asset, different returns are produced. For instance, a lot of equities pay dividends quarterly, whereas bonds often pay interest quarterly. Several forms of income are taxed at various rates in many jurisdictions.

Price appreciation is a significant part of the return in addition to regular income like dividends or interest. So, the total return on investment can be thought of as the sum of income and capital growth. According to Standard & Poor's estimates, dividends have made up about a third of the total equity return for the S&P 500 since 1926, while capital gains have made up the other two-thirds.

Thus, capital gains are a crucial component of investment.

Saving and investing are seen as two sides of the same coin by economists. This is so that the bank, which receives your savings when you deposit money there, can lend it to people or businesses who want to borrow it for legitimate purposes. As a result, your savings are frequently invested by someone else.

Different Investments

The majority of financial instruments used today to raise and invest funds in enterprises are referred to as investments. These businesses then rake that capital and put it to work expanding or making money.

Although there are many different sorts of investments, the following are the most typical ones:

Stocks

An investor who purchases stock in a corporation gains partial ownership of it. Shareholders are those who own a company's stock and can benefit from the company's expansion and success by increasing the value of their investment and receiving regular dividend payments from the company's earnings.

Bonds

Bonds are debt obligations of organizations like corporations, governments, and municipalities. A bond implies that you own a portion of a company's debt and are qualified to receive periodic interest payments as well as the face value of the bond once it matures.

Funds
Investment managers manage funds, which are pooled instruments that let investors buy stocks, bonds, preferred shares, commodities, etc. Mutual funds and exchange-traded funds, or ETFs, are two of the most popular categories of funds. ETFs trade on stock exchanges and, like stocks, are constantly valued throughout the trading day, unlike mutual funds, which do not trade on an exchange and are valued at the close of the trading day. Mutual funds and ETFs can be actively managed by fund managers or can passively track indices like the S&P 500 or the Dow Jones Industrial Average.

Securities Trusts
Another category of pooled investment is trusts. One of the most well-known types of securities in this group is real estate investment trusts

(REITs). REITs engage in residential or commercial real estate, and from the rental revenue generated by these properties, they distribute money to their investors regularly. Due to their trading on stock exchanges, REITs give their investors the benefit of immediate liquidity.

Alternative Investments
Hedge funds and private equity fall under the umbrella term of alternative investments. The reason why hedge funds are so named is that they can utilize long and short positions in stocks and other investments to diversify their investing bets. Without becoming public, private equity enables businesses to raise financing. Typically, wealthy individuals who met particular income and net worth standards and were referred to as "accredited investors" were the only ones with access to hedge funds and private equity. Alternative investments have, however, recently been made available to retail investors in fund formats.

Alternative Derivatives and Options

Financial instruments known as derivatives derive their value from another instrument, like a stock or index. Popular derivatives like options contracts provide the buyer the option, but not the duty, to purchase or sell a security at a specified price within a predetermined window of time. Leverage is frequently used in derivatives, making them a high-risk, high-reward investment.

Commodities
Along with financial instruments and currencies, commodities also include things like metals, oil, grains, and animal goods. Commodity futures, which are contracts to purchase or sell a specific amount of a commodity at a given price on a specific future date, or ETFs are the two ways they can be traded. Commodities can be traded for speculative or risk-hedging objectives.

Comparing Investment Approaches
Let's contrast a few of the most popular investing approaches:

Active versus passive investing: By actively managing the investment portfolio, active investing seeks to "beat the index." Contrarily, passive investing promotes a passive strategy, such as purchasing an index fund, as a tacit admission that it is challenging to continuously outperform the market. Both strategies have advantages and disadvantages, but in practice, only a few fund managers routinely outperform their benchmarks to make active management's higher costs worthwhile.

Value vs. Growth: Value firms often have lower price-earnings (P/E) ratios than high-growth corporations, which are preferred by growth investors. Because they may be out of favor with investors either temporarily or for an extended length of time, value investors seek out companies with PE ratios that are much lower than growth companies and greater dividend yields.

What to Invest In
Self-Directed Investment
The answer to the question "how to invest" depends on whether you are a Do-It-Yourself (DIY) type of investor or would rather have a

professional manage your money. Due to the low commissions and simplicity of trading on their platforms, many investors who prefer to handle their funds have accounts at discounts or online brokerages.

DIY investing, also known as self-directed investment, calls for a good deal of knowledge, expertise, time commitment, and emotional restraint. If you don't fit these descriptions, it could be a better idea to let a professional manage your money.

Investing Professionally Managed
Wealth managers typically handle investments for investors who seek professional money management. AUM, or assets under management, is the standard proportion that wealth managers charge their clients as their fee. Although though hiring a professional money manager costs more than managing money on one's own, some investors are willing to pay for the ease of having an expert handle the research, investment decisions, and trading.

Investors are urged by the SEC's Office of Investor Education and Advocacy to verify that their investment professional is registered and licensed.

Robotic investment advice

Some investors decide which investments to make based on advice from computerized financial consultants. Roboadvisors, which use algorithms and artificial intelligence to generate recommendations, compile vital data about the investor and their risk profile. Roboadvisors, which operate with little to no human intervention, provide services akin to those of a human investment advisor at a lower cost. With technological developments, roboadvisors can now do more than just choose assets. They can aid in the creation of retirement plans as well as the administration of trusts and other retirement accounts like 401(k)s.

A Synopsis of Investment History

Although the idea of investing has been around for thousands of years, the modern form of investing can be traced back to the 17th and 18th centuries, when the first public markets were created and investors were introduced to investment options. The New York Stock Exchange (NYSE) and the Amsterdam Stock Exchange were both founded in 1602 and 1792, respectively.

Investing in the Industrial Revolution
Greater affluence brought about by the Industrial Revolutions of 1760–1840 and 1860–1914 led to an increase in savings that could be invested, which encouraged the growth of a sophisticated banking system. The majority of the well-known institutions that currently rule the world of investment, such as Goldman Sachs and J.P. Morgan.

The 20th Century of Investment
With the creation of novel ideas in asset pricing, portfolio theory, and risk management, the 20th century saw significant advancements in investing theory. Hedge funds, private equity, venture capital, REITs, and ETFs are just a few of the numerous new investment vehicles that were launched in the second half of the 20th century.

The Internet's explosive growth in the 1990s opened up online trading and research to the general public, completing the democratization of investment that had begun more than a century earlier.

Contemporary Investment
The dot.com boom, which produced a new generation of billionaires from investments in stocks of technology-driven and internet businesses, burst around the beginning of the twenty-first century and may have set the stage for future events. The collapse of Enron in 2001 captured the public's attention with its brazen exhibition of deceit that left the business, its accounting firm, Arthur Andersen, and many of its investors bankrupt.

The Great Recession (2007–2009) that crippled economies all over the world as a result of a vast number of failed investments in mortgage-backed securities is one of the most notable events of the twenty-first century or history for that matter. Famous banks and investment companies failed, foreclosures increased, and the wealth disparity grew.

By flooding the market with low-cost online investment firms and free trading apps like Robinhood, the 21st century also made investing accessible to beginners and unconventional investors.

Investing vs. Speculation

Three elements determine whether purchasing a security counts as investing or speculating:

The level of risk assumed: Compared to speculating, investing often entails a lesser level of risk.

The investment's holding term: Investment normally has a longer holding period, which is frequently measured in years, whereas speculation typically has considerably shorter holding periods.

Source of returns: Dividends or distributions may make up a sizable portion of investment returns while price appreciation may be a relatively minor one. Price growth typically represents the primary source of returns in speculating.

A stable blue chip is far less risky than a cryptocurrency because price volatility is a standard metric of risk. Hence, purchasing a dividend-paying blue chip with the intent to retain it for several years would be considered investing. But, a trader who purchases a cryptocurrency to sell it for a profit in a matter of days is engaging in speculation.

An illustration of investment return
Let's say you paid $310 for 100 shares of the XYZ stock and sold it for $460.20 exactly one year later. Without commissions, what was your approximate total return? Remember that XYZ doesn't distribute stock dividends. A capital gain of (($460.20 - $310.)/$310) x 100% = 48.5% would result.

Imagine that XYZ had paid out $5 in dividends per share during the time you held the company's stock. The sum of your approximate total return (capital gains: 48.5% + dividends: ($500/$31,000) x 100% = 1.61%) would be 50.11 percent.

Where Should I Begin Investing?

You have two options for investing: you may do it yourself and choose investments based on your investing style, or you can work with a professional, like a broker or advisor. It's crucial to ascertain your preferences and risk tolerance before investing. Stocks and options may not be the ideal choice if you are risk-averse. Create a plan detailing how much, how frequently, and in what to invest based on objectives and preferences. Be sure the target investment is in line with your plan and can produce the required results before committing to your resources. Don't forget that you don't need a lot of money to start, and you can adapt as your needs do.

What Kinds of Investments Are There?
There are numerous investment options available. The most popular ones are probably equities, bonds, property, and ETFs/mutual funds. Real estate, certificates of deposit, annuities, cryptocurrencies, commodities, collectibles, and precious metals are more investment options to think about.

How Can Invest Help My Funds Grow?

Investments are not only for the wealthy. You can make little investments. You may, for instance, buy inexpensive stocks, put tiny sums of money into a savings account that pays interest, or save up until you have the desired sum to invest. Save aside small sums from your pay if your employer provides a retirement plan, such as a 401(k), until you can increase your investment. Your investment might have doubled if your employer takes part in matching programs.

You might start buying stocks, bonds, mutual funds, or even an IRA. $1,000 is hardly a little investment, to begin with. In 1997, a $1,000 investment in Amazon's IPO would now be worth millions. This was mostly caused by several stock splits, but the outcome—impressive returns—remains the same. Most financial organizations provide savings accounts, which often don't require a sizable investment. Go around to discover a savings account with the best features and the most affordable rates as savings accounts don't often offer large interest rates.

Unbelievable as it may seem, $1,000 can be used to purchase real estate. Although you might not be able to purchase an investment property, you can invest in a business that does. A business that invests in and manages real estate to increase profits and generate income is known as a real estate investment trust (REIT). You can buy REIT stocks, mutual funds, or exchange-traded vehicles for $1,000.

Are investing and gambling the same thing?
Yes, gambling and investing are very different. When you invest, you put your money to work in ventures or pursuits that have positive expected returns, or returns that will be positive in the long run. Betting on the results of events or games is referred to as gambling. Nothing is being done with your money. Gambling frequently has a low expected return. Investments can lose money, but only if the project they are part of falls short of expectations. Contrarily, gambling results are entirely determined by chance.

In conclusion

The act of investing involves putting money into something to make money or make a profit. The type of investment you select may depend on your goals for the money and your risk tolerance. In general, taking on fewer risks results in lower returns, whereas taking on more risks results in higher returns. Stocks, bonds, real estate, precious metals, and other assets can all be invested in. One can invest using cash, assets, digital currencies, or other forms of trade.

The risks and benefits associated with various investment vehicles, including stocks, bonds, mutual funds, and real estate, vary.

Investors have two options: they can invest on their own, without the assistance of a financial expert, or they can hire a qualified and registered investment advisor. Also, investors now have the option of using roboadvisors to receive automated investment solutions.

The sum of money required for an investment mostly relies on the type of investment as well as the investor's financial situation, objectives, and aspirations. The minimum investment criteria for many vehicles have been reduced, nevertheless, making participation more accessible to more people.

Research your aim as well as your investment manager or platform, regardless of how or what you decide to invest in. Warren Buffet, a seasoned and successful investor, once said, "Never invest in a firm you cannot comprehend." This may be one of the best pearls of wisdom.

Building a diversified investment portfolio

It appears nearly impossible to sell a stock for any amount less than the price you paid when the market is flourishing. We must remember the significance of a well-diversified portfolio in every market scenario, though, as we can never be certain of what the market will do at any one time.

The investment community preaches the same thing the real estate market promotes for buying a house: "location, location, location." In other words, you should never put all your eggs in one basket when developing an investing plan that limits possible losses in a down market. The idea of diversity is based on this core tenet.

Continue reading for information on the benefits of diversification for your portfolio as well as advice on how to choose wisely.

Why Diversify Your Portfolio?
Many financial advisers, fund managers, and individual investors alike advocate for diversification. It is a portfolio management strategy that combines many investments. Diversifying your investments is meant to increase your return on investment. It also implies that choosing multiple investment vehicles will reduce the risk for investors.

Strategies for Diversifying Your Investments
The idea of diversification is not new. We may review the market gyrations and responses as they started to falter during the dotcom crash, the Great Recession, and once more during the

COVID-19 recession with the benefit of hindsight.

Remembering that investing is an art form rather than a reflex activity, we should begin practicing disciplined investing with a diverse portfolio before it becomes essential. 80% of the harm has already been done by the time the typical investor "reacts" to the market. A well-diversified portfolio with an investing horizon of at least five years can weather most storms in this situation, more so than in most others.

Here are five suggestions to aid in your diversification:

1. Share Your Wealth
Stocks might be great, but you shouldn't invest all of your money in a single stock or industry. Try investing in a few companies you are familiar with, have faith in, and perhaps even use regularly to build your virtual mutual fund.

Stocks, however, are not the only factor to take into account. Commodities, exchange-traded funds (ETFs), and real estate investment trusts are other investing options (REITs). Moreover, venture beyond your base of operations. Go beyond it and consider the world. You will distribute your risk in this manner, which may result in greater benefits.

Some would say that sticking with what you know will make the average investor too focused on retail, yet getting to know a firm or using its products and services can be a wholesome and healthy way to approach this industry.

Don't, however, make the mistake of going too far. Make sure you limit your portfolio to something you can handle. When you don't have the time or money to keep up, there's no point in investing in 100 different automobiles. Strive to keep your investment portfolio to 20 to 30 distinct ones.

2. Think about bond or index funds.
You might want to think about including fixed-income funds or index funds in the mix. Securities tracking several indices are a great

long-term investment for portfolio diversification. You can further insure your portfolio against market volatility and unpredictability by adding some fixed-income products. Instead of investing in a particular industry, these funds aim to replicate the performance of broad indexes by trying to capture the value of the bond market.

Another benefit of these funds is that they frequently have cheap costs. More money in your pocket as a result. Due to the low overhead required to operate these funds, there are also no administration or operational expenses.

The fact that index funds are passively managed may be a disadvantage. Although passive investing often costs less, it might nonetheless perform poorly in unfavorable market conditions. In fixed-income markets, for instance, active management can be advantageous, particularly in trying economic times.

3. Continue to expand your portfolio.

Regularly increase your investment amounts. When investing $10,000, employ dollar-cost averaging. The peaks and troughs caused by market volatility are lessened with the use of this strategy. This strategy's goal is to lower your investment risk by making the same amount of investments over time.

You put money into a certain portfolio of securities regularly when you use dollar-cost averaging. While using this method, you would purchase more shares at low prices and fewer at high prices.

4. Recognize when to leave

Both dollar-cost averaging and buying and holding are sensible tactics. But, just because your investments are running automatically doesn't imply you should disregard the factors at play.

Keep your investments up to date and informed of any shifts in the state of the market as a whole. You'll want to be aware of the state of the businesses you invest in. You'll be able to determine when to sell, take a loss, and move on to your next investment by doing this as well.

5. Keep an eye out for commissions
Understand what you are getting for the fees you are paying if you are not the trading type. While some businesses impose monthly fees, others impose transactional costs. They can build up and seriously hurt your bottom line.

Be conscious of the price you are paying and the value you are receiving. Do not forget that the cheapest option is not necessarily the best. Keep yourself informed if there are any fee adjustments.

This aspect is less of a worry today because many online brokers now offer commission-free trading in many stocks and ETFs for $0. Nonetheless, there are still frequent fees associated with trading mutual funds, illiquid stocks, and alternative asset classes.

Why Do I Need to Diversify?
Investors who diversify their portfolios avoid "putting all of their eggs in one basket."

According to the theory, if one stock, industry, or asset class declines, others can increase. This is particularly true if the securities or assets held do not have a high degree of correlation. Diversification reduces the portfolio's overall risk mathematically without lowering the projected return.

Are Index Funds Diverse Enough?
An index fund or ETF mimics an index by definition. The degree of diversification may vary depending on the index. For instance, the Dow Jones Industrial Average contains only 30 stock components compared to the S&P 500's more than 500, making the latter much less diversified.

Even if you own an S&P 500 index fund, your portfolio may not be sufficiently diversified if you don't also have moderate allocations in low-correlation asset classes including bonds, commodities, real estate, and alternative investments, among others.

Can a Portfolio Be Over-Diversified?

Yes. The objectives of diversification are not met if adding a new investment to a portfolio raises its overall risk and/or lowers its projected return (without lowering the risk appropriately). When a portfolio has the appropriate amount of stocks or when you add closely correlated securities, this "over-diversification" is more likely to occur.

How Is the Risk of a Portfolio Measured?
The overall standard deviation of returns serves as a proxy for the risk of a diversified portfolio. The predicted riskiness increases as the standard deviation increases.

In conclusion
Investing should and may be enjoyable. It may be instructive, enlightening, and satisfying. You may find investing beneficial even in the worst of circumstances by adopting a disciplined strategy and utilizing diversification, buy-and-hold, and dollar-cost averaging tactics.

Minimizing risk and maximizing returns

maximizing profits and reducing risk

How can you run your firm to maximize profits while minimizing risk? This million-dollar query has everyone interested in finding out the solution. It is true that, for the most part, accumulation requires speculating. The danger associated with speculating differs, though. You must remove as much risk from speculating as you can if you want your firm to grow. You contain the risk ratio when you have control over it.

For instance, while analyzing stock and share movement, financial professionals may use Roger Khoury's "Market Vulnerability Analysis" to assess any speculative move. By doing this, individuals increase their sense of control, objectivity, and confidence in their abilities to analyze markets and price movement and forecast risk as it grows and shrinks. The Transition Guy's podcast included Roger Khoury as a special guest. We can utilize the same framework as business executives to grow and invest in our companies.

You are not required to enter or exit.

It doesn't necessarily follow that increasing risk entails increasing reward. You are capable of making thoughtful, well-informed judgments for your company. For instance, while making those crucial business decisions, take the time to weigh your company's goals against a potentially unfavorable outcome. Make sure you can handle any negative consequences of your decisions.

You can reduce your downside market risk without reducing your possibility for profit, similar to the Market Vulnerability Analysis. You must consider the market while making judgments and work with it. It's also crucial to maintain composure when making significant judgments.

For instance, you might decide to expand your workforce by 5 people. This won't immediately result in more profits because you'll need to train your team, which takes time. The operation will take some time. You must give changes and decisions time to take effect, though.

Make wise selections based on your knowledge. Before making significant business decisions, you must conduct due diligence. You must make sure your choices can endure any market fluctuation if the market is turbulent, as it is right now because of the pandemic. For instance, you might need to decide whether to change the direction of your company and go online. If you want to go online, think about whether getting rid of your physical facility can help you save money on setup charges. Make sure the risk is balanced. Going down the road might not be a good idea if it is too high.

Always take your environment into account. A market responds to its surroundings. We must first take into account the market we are operating in when making decisions that will have an impact on the operation of our firm. What has an impact on it? Is the political climate steady, or will there be the talk of changes that could impact what we have to offer? What position does your specific product occupy in the market, and would that position alter if the market moves? The weather may be predicted. We can measure specific weather fronts, and we know that they will produce clouds and rain.

When rain is predicted, we are aware that we will need an umbrella to stay dry. We can change our plans for the day if it is predicted to rain heavily; this also applies to business.

You must be able to lead your company effectively in both good and poor weather. Forecasting is therefore crucial. Instead of concentrating on just one component of your surroundings, take into account all the variables that could affect the market and incorporate them into your forecast. Raise the wave, but be aware of its general shape.

The results of business decisions are never certain.
Something is not always a sure thing just because you can predict it. It makes sense not to move forward at that time if the market appears to be against your business goal. Alternatively, start over or take a new path. Make sure your decision is one you are over 80% confident about. Control the danger. It

might not be the best choice if it is unlikely to yield significant benefits for you in the long run. When making decisions, be devoid of emotion and impartial.

Avoid making rash decisions.
No matter how brilliant a decision-maker you are, you will usually make bad decisions if you are under pressure and stress. It is comparable to operating a vehicle late. You are familiar with the laws of the road and how to operate a car. Yet when you're under pressure, you'll drive the automobile differently; you might drive more aggressively to get there faster, and the hazards significantly rise.

You might be ticketed, hurt someone in an accident or both. If we are under pressure, we frequently feel as though we must act rapidly in business. As a company leader, the ability to make judgments is crucial, but these decisions need to be well-informed and understood.

The secret to reducing risk and maximizing return is consistency and meticulous application.

Put less emphasis on getting money rapidly. The process that produces a specific set of results should be the center of attention. Additionally, you can beat the market you're in and make money for your company by applying constancy and diligence.

What is Return Maximization?
The term "maximizing return" is frequently used in the business world. It entails maximizing your resources to get the most return on your investment. There are several approaches to maximize return but often entail raising sales while cutting costs.

How much return you can expect on your investment depends on several things. The level of danger involved is typically the most important factor. The rewards on higher-risk investments are often larger, but the danger of loss is generally higher. Hence, before making any investments, it is crucial to carefully examine your risk tolerance.

The length of time you anticipate earning it also affects your return. Although they carry less risk, short-term investments often have smaller returns than long-term ones. It can be worthwhile to accept a lower return if you require the money sooner.

Ultimately, your return will depend on how much money you have to invest. The potential return increases with the amount of money invested. Only invest, nevertheless, what you can afford to lose without jeopardizing your financial stability.

In business and investing, maximizing return is a key idea. Making ensuring you consistently consider risk and reward is important. You can make sure you are getting the most out of your investment and accomplishing your financial goals by carefully weighing all the aspects involved.

How Do You Maximize Return on Investment?
There are numerous strategies to increase return on investment (ROI). Yet in the end, it all boils down to making sure you receive the most value for your money.

How much money you're producing compared to how much money you're spending is one way to think about return on investment (ROI). If you're earning more than you're spending, you're doing fairly well. Yet, you need to rethink your approach if your expenses are outpacing your income.

How much value you are creating in comparison to how much value you are destroying is another method to consider ROI. This is frequently known as the "value-add" strategy. If you're adding more value than you're taking away, you're doing quite well. But if you're erasing more value than you're adding, you need to rethink your approach.

Naturally, ROI is not the only factor to consider. There are more things to think about. Yet, if you want to increase your chances of success, concentrate on making the most of your money. Also, never forget to look at the big picture.

What does reducing risk mean?

The process of discovering, evaluating, and controlling hazards is known as risk management. It is a proactive strategy that aids businesses in reducing losses and maximizing opportunities.

Risk management consists of these three essential elements:

1. The first stage in risk management is identification. Organizations must determine the dangers they are exposed to. Many techniques, including focus groups, interviews, questionnaires, and surveys, can be used to accomplish this.

2. Risk assessment is necessary when risks have been discovered to determine their impact and likelihood. This will assist companies in prioritizing which dangers require immediate attention.

3. Control - Implementing controls to reduce or eliminate the risks that have been identified is the last step in risk management. This could involve implementing new technology,

changing regulations and processes, or implementing training programs.

The overarching strategy of every firm must include risk management. Understanding the various risk types and the threats related to them is essential. Organizations may reduce losses and increase opportunities by being proactive.

What is the Best Investment Risk Minimization Strategy?
The subject of how to reduce risk when investing does not have a single solution. Because every individual's circumstances are different, what works for one investor could not work for another.

Having said that, several fundamental ideas can lower risk for all investors. One strategy is to spread out your investments among various asset classes. This entails investing your money in a variety of financial instruments, including stocks, bonds, and real estate. Spreading your money around will boost your chances of reaching your financial objectives by preventing you from putting all of your financial eggs in one basket.

Long-term investing is another strategy to lower risk. This increases your likelihood of surviving any short-term market turbulence and ultimately achieving your objectives.

Of course, no plan is without risk. Yet by adhering to these guidelines, you can lessen your risk and improve your chances of succeeding financially.

There is some risk associated with investing, including the potential loss of money. Any strategy has no assurance that it will be effective. Diversification does not guarantee success or offer protection from loss in weak markets. Long-term investing does not guarantee a profit in the short term and may cause you to miss out on market chances during that time. Future outcomes cannot be predicted based on past performance, and results can change over time. Please discuss your case with a reputable financial counselor.

Contact me or visit my podcast, Optimizing Returns And Reducing Risks, for more information on how to make the best decisions to advance your business.

How should returns be maximized?
Achieving the highest possible return on investment is what is meant by "maximizing returns" (ROI). There are several ways to accomplish this, including:

Buying high-growth stocks: These are stocks with the potential to produce big long-term returns.
Purchasing dividend stocks: Dividend stocks are a great option for investors aiming to maximize returns because they frequently outperform the market over the long term.
Reinvesting dividends is a fantastic method to boost your earnings over time. Reinvesting your dividends is like giving yourself a raise, which can hasten the achievement of your financial objectives.

Holding for the long term: Just holding onto your various investments for the long run is one of the finest methods to optimize your returns. By doing this, you'll give them time to compound and expand, which might result in large profits.

One of the most crucial things you can do as an investor is to diversify your portfolio. You can reduce your risk of any one asset allocation losing value by investing across a range of asset classes.

Using dollar-cost averaging: Dollar-cost averaging is an excellent method for lowering investment risk. You can smooth out market fluctuations and avoid making purchases at excessive prices by consistently investing a set amount of money into a security.

Investing in index funds: Using index funds to diversify your portfolio is easy and efficient. You can increase your returns by investing in an index fund, which will expose you to a wide range of stocks.

Exchange-traded funds (ETFs) are an easy and efficient approach to diversifying an investment portfolio. ETFs follow a wide range of indices, which can aid in maximizing return.

Leverage is a useful instrument that may help you maximize your results. Your chances of making money investing might be increased by taking out a loan (or losses). Leverage can raise the likelihood of losing money, therefore it's crucial to utilize it carefully.

Using a disciplined investing approach: A disciplined approach is essential for long-term success. You'll have a better chance of succeeding if you adhere to your strategy and restrain your emotions.

How does diversity help us reduce risks?
Diversification is essential for reducing risk. You may diversify your investments to spread your risk and guard against any losses.

Diversifying can be done in a few different ways. Investing in various asset types, such as stocks, bonds, and cash, is one approach. Investing in other industries, such as healthcare, technology, and consumer products, is another option. Finally, you may diversify geographically by investing in businesses from other nations throughout the world.

Your unique aims and objectives will determine the optimal strategy for diversification. Diversification is one of the most crucial things you can do to reduce portfolio risk and preserve your portfolio, regardless of how you go about it.

Diversification is essential for reducing risk. You may diversify your investments to spread your risk and guard against any losses.

How may the risk associated with your investment be reduced?
There are a few important strategies to reduce risk in your investment:

1. Increase portfolio diversity.

Keep your diversification in mind. To lower your portfolio's overall risk, distribute your assets among a variety of asset classes and industry sectors.

2. Regularly review your investments.

Make careful to monitor the performance of your investment portfolio and readjust as necessary. This will assist you in staying on course and minimizing unnecessary danger.

3. Maintain your investing strategy's discipline.

Don't allow feelings to influence your choices. Maintain your path and resist being influenced by market gyrations.

You may assist reduce investment risk and maintain the direction of your portfolio by heeding this important advice.

Keep in mind that failure to learn is learning failure.

CHAPTER 4:

BUILDING PASSIVE INCOME STREAMS

Whether you're attempting to start a side business or are just looking to make a little more money each month, passive income may be a wonderful approach to help you produce extra cash flow. This is especially true now that the economy is experiencing widespread inflation. When things are good, passive income may help you make more money. It can also help you get by if you suddenly lose your job, decide to take time off work, or if inflation keeps eating away at your purchasing power.

With passive income, you can continue to make money while working at your regular job or, if you're able to establish a reliable passive income stream, you may wish to take a little time off. A passive income provides you additional security in any case.

The idea of creating wealth through passive income may also appeal to you if you're concerned about being able to save enough of your salary to achieve your retirement objectives.

Ideas for passive income

Develop a course
Produce an ebook
Rental revenue
Affiliate promotion
Flipping retail goods
Online photography sales
Acquire real estate using crowdsourcing
Interpersonal lending
stock dividends
Make an app
Lease a parking spot
REITs
a ladder of bonds
social media-sponsored posts
Consider opening a high-yield saving or a CD.
Renting out your house temporarily
Promote on your vehicle
Publish a blog or a YouTube channel.
Rent out practical home goods
Provide designs online

Create an annuity
Purchase a local company
Get a blog.

Passive income: What is it?
Regular profits from a source other than an employer or contractor are considered passive income. According to the Internal Revenue Service (IRS), passive income can originate from either rental property or a company in which a person is not actively involved, such as receiving stock dividends or book royalties.

It has a "get-rich-quick" allure, but in the end, it still requires labor. Many people believe that passive income is about receiving something for nothing. You only provide the labor upfront.

In reality, you might accomplish all or some of the work upfront, but passive income frequently requires some more work along the road as well. To keep the passive income coming in, you might need to keep your product updated or your rental property well-maintained.

But if you stick with the plan, it may be a terrific method to make money and you'll gain some more financial stability along the road.

It's not passive income.

You're duty. Generally speaking, passive income is not money that you have directly participated in, such as salary from a job.

another employment. Taking up a second job won't count as a passive income source because you'll still have to put in the time and effort to get rewarded for it. Creating a steady stream of money without putting in a lot of effort is what passive income is all about.

assets that don't generate income. If you own assets that produce dividends or interest, investing might be a terrific method to create passive income. While stocks or other investments that don't pay dividends, such as cryptocurrencies, may be intriguing, they don't produce passive income.

23 wealth-building passive income ideas

Check out these 23 tactics if you're considering establishing a passive income stream, and discover what it takes to be successful with each one while also being aware of the hazards involved.

1. Develop a course

Making an audio or video course, then sitting back and watching the money stream in from the sale of your product, is a common method for generating passive income. Sites like Udemy, SkillShare, and Coursera allow for the distribution and sale of courses.

A "freemium model" is an alternative that entails gaining a following through free material and then charging for in-depth knowledge or for people who want to know more. This paradigm may be used, for instance, by language instructors and stock-picking counsel. The free material serves as an example of your skills and could draw individuals seeking advancement.

Opportunity: A course may generate a fantastic revenue stream since, after the first-time investment, earning money is simple.

Risk: "The product requires a tremendous amount of work to create," And it needs to be excellent to generate good revenue. There is no place for trash outside.

If you want to be successful, you must create a solid platform, market your products, and make plans for additional products.

"Unless you are incredibly lucky, one product is not a business," "Creating additional top-notch items is the best approach to increase sales of an existing product."

You can create a reliable income stream once you have mastered the company strategy.

2. Produce an ebook

Creating an e-book can be a smart way to benefit from the cheap cost of publication and even use Amazon's global distribution to bring your book in front of possibly millions of prospective customers. Since they rely on your skills, e-books may be created for relatively little money and lengths of 30 to 50 pages.

You'll need to be an authority on a certain subject, although it's possible that the subject is narrow and calls for specialized knowledge or talents that few possess but that many people desire. With an online platform, you can quickly create the book and test-market several titles and pricing points.

Nevertheless, most of the value comes when you include more e-books in the mix, bringing in more readers to your material, much as when developing a course.

Opportunity: An e-book may serve as a vehicle for directing readers to your other products, such as audio or video courses, additional e-books, a website, or perhaps more valuable seminars, in addition to providing them with useful information and value.

Risk: Your e-book needs to be excellent to get readers, and it also helps if you have a marketing strategy in place, such as a website that already exists, a promotion on other related websites, media appearances, podcasts, or something else. Hence, you can put in a lot of labor upfront and receive little in return, especially initially.

Even while an e-book is good, it will assist if you write more and eventually create a company around it or make the book only one aspect of your company that supports the others. So, your greatest risk is usually wasting your time for little gain.

3. Rental revenue

Renting out real estate is a good strategy to generate passive income. Yet more effort than individuals anticipates is frequently required.

You risk losing your entire investment if you don't take the time to understand how to make it lucrative.

Opportunity: You must decide on three factors to getting passive income from rental properties:

Your desired rate of return on investment
The overall costs and expenses for the property
The costs associated with owning the property

You would need to charge $3,133 in monthly rent to meet your objective, for instance, if you aim to generate $10,000 a year in rental cash flow and the property has a $2,000 monthly mortgage plus an additional $300 a month in taxes and other expenditures.

Risk: A few things to think about include: Is there a market for your property? What if you rent to someone who makes late payments or mistreats the property? What if you can't get a tenant for your property? Any one of these elements might significantly reduce your passive income.

Moreover, economic turbulence might provide difficulties. You can find yourself with renters who are suddenly unable to pay their rent while you still have your mortgage to pay. Nevertheless, if revenues fall, you might not be able to rent the house out for as much as you once could. However, rentals might not be sufficient to cover your costs given that property prices have been growing swiftly, partly as a result of the historically low mortgage rates. To protect yourself, you should consider these dangers and have backup strategies in place.

4. Affiliate promotion

By the use of a link on their website or social media account, bloggers, social media "influencers," or proprietors of websites can promote a third party's product. The most well-known affiliate partner maybe Amazon, but other well-known brands include eBay, Awin, and ShareASale. Yet for companies trying to build a following and advertise their wares, Instagram and TikTok have grown into enormous platforms.

To bring attention to your blog or otherwise point people toward goods and services they might need, you can also think about building an email list.

Possibility: The website owner gains a commission when a visitor clicks on the link and buys anything from the third-party affiliate. As the commission might be between 3 and 7 percent, it will probably require a lot of visitors to your site to make any meaningful money. But, if you can expand your audience or find a lucrative specialty (like software, financial services, or fitness), you could be able to earn a sizable sum of money.

Because you might theoretically make money by just posting a link to your website or social media account, affiliate marketing is seen as passive. In actuality, you won't make any money if you can't get visitors to your website who will click on the link and make a purchase.

Risk: If you're just getting started, it will take time to produce content and increase visitors. Developing a following can take a long time, and finding the ideal recipe to draw in that audience will also likely take some time. Even worse, after all that effort, your audience can decide to go to the next well-liked influencer, fashion, or social media site.

5. Flipping retail goods
Use internet marketplaces like eBay or Amazon to your advantage and resell items you discover elsewhere for a discount. You can make money

by arbitraging the difference between your purchase and sell prices, and you can even develop a following of people who keep watch of your transactions.

A chance will present itself for you to profit from pricing variations between what you can find and what the typical consumer would be able to find. If you have a contact who can provide you access to inexpensive goods that few other people can locate, this may work very well for you. Or perhaps you can locate precious goods that others have merely missed.

Risk: Although internet transactions can occur at any moment, making this technique passive, you'll undoubtedly need to put in some extra effort to identify a trustworthy supplier of goods. Also, you'll need a reliable source of funding because you'll need to spend money on each of your items until they do sell. You'll need to be well-versed in the industry to avoid making an overpriced purchase. Otherwise, you can find yourself with goods that no one wants or whose price you need to slash significantly to sell.

6. Online photography sales

Although selling photography online might not seem like the most apparent way to start a passive income stream, you could be able to grow your efforts if you can sell the same images repeatedly. You may collaborate with a company like Getty Images, Shutterstock, or Alamy to do that.

You must first receive platform approval before you can start licensing your images for usage by anybody who downloads them. When someone uses your photo on the site, you get paid.

You'll need images that speak to a certain demographic or capture a particular scenario, and you'll need to figure out where the market is. Photographs might be of models, scenery, imaginative scenes, and more, or they could record actual occurrences that might be covered by the media.

Opportunity: If you can produce images that will be in demand, selling or licensing your photos through a platform gives you the chance to grow your efforts. It implies that you could be able to sell the same photograph hundreds, thousands, or even more times.

Risk: It's possible that after uploading hundreds of images to a platform like Getty Images, none of them will result in any sales that matter. You need to keep uploading photographs while you look for that one shot that will be the source of all of your money.

Going out and taking pictures, processing them, and staying up to date with events that can ultimately be the source of your earnings might all take a lot of work. Moreover, motivation may be difficult to maintain: Although it's unlikely, every subsequent shot may be your winning ticket in the lottery.

7. Acquire real estate using crowdsourcing
A crowdfunding site is another alternative if you want to invest in real estate but don't want to do a lot of the labor-intensive tasks (maintenance, repairs, dealing with renters, and more). Real estate is chosen by a skilled investing team, after which you can decide

whether to invest in it and how much you feel comfortable with.

The real estate platform would charge you a yearly management fee, and your initial investments might be as little as $10 or as much as $100,000.

Opportunity: You can have access to private real estate projects that experienced investors have preselected and that may be interesting. You may look at the returns on the platforms to have a better understanding of the kind of returns you can anticipate and for how long. Adding real estate assets to your portfolio might also assist to diversify it and evening out your earnings.

Although some platforms invest in debt, others do so in equity (stock). Debt often gives lower returns for less risk, whereas stocks typically offer higher returns for more risk. Some platforms demand that you have a minimum amount of assets or income, as well as be an authorized investor. Platforms like Fundrise,

Yieldstreet, and DiversyFund are well-liked options.

Risk: Several crowdfunding websites require you to make your investments. The results of the past, while they may appear positive, do not guarantee future success. You'll also need to use your judgment while deciding what to buy. As a result, you must examine the prospectus for any transaction you're considering and comprehend its advantages and disadvantages.

Real estate is also frequently financed with substantial amounts of debt, which makes it more vulnerable to any downturn in the economy. Also, especially in an emergency, you should be aware of how long your money will be locked up in the investment and when you may retrieve it.

8. Interpersonal lending

Peer-to-peer (P2P) loans are private loans arranged between you and a borrower via a third-party middleman, like Prosper. Other companies include Payoff, which targets better credit risks, and Funding Circle, which targets corporations and offers bigger borrowing limits.

Opportunity: As a lender, you may make money by collecting interest on the loans. But, because the loan is unsecured, a default might leave you with nothing.

You must take two steps to reduce that risk:

By spreading out smaller sums of money across many loans, you may diversify your lending portfolio. The minimum loan investment at Prosper.com is $25.

To make wise decisions, examine the prospective borrowers' historical data.

Risk: As P2P lending is not 100% passive and requires time to understand the metrics, you need thoroughly vet your potential borrowers. You must closely monitor payments because you are investing in several loans. If you want to increase your income, you should reinvest whatever interest you earn.

High-yielding personal loans may also be more prone to fail during economic downturns;

hence, when things become worse economically, these loans may default at larger rates than usual.

9. stock dividends
Companies with dividend-paying stocks make payments repeatedly to their shareholders. All you need to do to receive cash dividends from a company is own the stock. Businesses pay them out quarterly from their profits. The more shares you hold, the bigger your payment will be since dividends are paid per share of stock.

Opportunity: Owning dividend-paying stocks can be one of the most passive ways to make money because the income from the stocks is unrelated to any action outside the original financial investment. Simply put, the funds will be placed into your brokerage account.

Risk: Choosing the correct investments is difficult.

Companies that pay out excessively high dividends, for instance, might not be able to maintain them. A disproportionate number of newcomers enter the market without fully researching the firm issuing the shares. You need to familiarize yourself with each company's financial statements and conduct further research on their websites. "You should investigate each firm for two to three weeks."

Nonetheless, there are methods to invest in dividend-paying stocks without investing a lot of time in company research. ETFs, or exchange-traded funds, are a superior choice. ETFs are investment vehicles that contain bonds, commodities, and equities but trade similarly to stocks. ETFs also help you diversify your assets, so if one firm reduces its dividend, it won't have a significant impact on the ETF's price or income. Here are some of the top ETFs available.

"ETFs are a great option for beginners since they are simple to comprehend, extremely liquid, affordable, and offer significantly higher potential returns due to far lower fees than mutual funds.

Another major danger is that stocks or ETFs might decline considerably over brief periods, particularly in unpredictable times like the financial markets' shocker in 2020 caused by the coronavirus epidemic. While diversified funds may experience less of a squeeze, economic hardship can nevertheless lead to certain corporations completely reducing their payouts.

Use the brokerage reviews on Bankrate to compare your investment alternatives.

10. Make an app

Making the first-time commitment to creating an app may allow you to later reap the benefits. Your app may be a game or a tool that makes it easier for mobile users to carry out a challenging task. After your software is available to the public, consumers may download it and you can make money.

Opportunity: If you can create an app that appeals to your audience, it has a lot of potentials. You must think about the best way to make your app profitable. For instance, you may display in-app advertisements or charge a small fee to customers to download the app.

To maintain the app's appeal and relevancy when it grows in popularity or as a result of user input, you'll probably need to add little additions.

Risk: Using your time inefficiently is perhaps the largest danger in this situation. There is no financial risk involved if you invest little to no money in the project (or money that you would have spent on hardware, for example). It's a saturated business, though, and applications that succeed must provide consumers with a compelling value or experience.

Also, you should confirm that your app complies with local privacy regulations if it gathers any data, as these rules vary from country to country. However, app success might be fleeting, which means your income flow could run out far quicker than you anticipate.

11. Hire a parking spot

Have you have a parking spot that you're not using or that someone else might use? The area might be exchanged for money. It might be an even better setup if you have a bigger space that can accommodate several cars or that can be used for a variety of events or venues.

Opportunity: Your parking spot might be worth real money in areas or times with high demand (such as during a concert or sporting event). For instance, you might have a money-maker on your hands if you live close to a location with frequent commuters but is short on parking spaces. Renting to someone who requires the space daily, as opposed to for one-time events, may give you the best chance of making a profit.

Risk: Although renting out a parking space may not be particularly risky, you should make sure you are not infringing on any rules from your residence or any other entity. A liability disclaimer as a prerequisite for using your spot should probably be included as well.

12. REITs

Real estate investment trusts (REITs) are a fancy name for businesses that own and manage real estate. Since they pass the majority of their income on to shareholders, REITs have a unique legal structure that allows them to pay little to no corporate income tax.

Opportunity: REITs are just like any other company or dividend stock in that you can buy them on the stock market. You will receive whatever the REIT pays out in dividends, and since the best REITs typically increase their dividend on an annual basis, you may eventually accrue a growing stream of dividends.

Individual REIT ownership can carry more risk than investing in an ETF that holds multiple REIT stocks, much like dividend stocks. A fund offers instant diversification, is typically much safer than buying individual stocks, and still provides a nice return.

Risk: Selecting high-quality REITs requires the same skills as selecting dividend stocks; this calls for a thorough analysis of each potential purchase candidate. Even though it's a passive activity, if you don't know what you're doing, you could lose a lot of money. Like any stock, the price is subject to significant short-term fluctuations.

Dividends from REITs are also not immune to a downturn in the economy. The REIT will probably have to reduce or stop paying a dividend if it doesn't make enough money. Therefore, your passive income could be affected just when you need it most.

13. a ladder of bonds

A bond ladder is a collection of bonds that mature over several years at various times. The risk of reinvesting your money when bonds offer too-low interest payments can be reduced thanks to the staggered maturities.

Opportunity: Bond ladders are a traditional passive investment that has long been popular among retirees and those who are approaching retirement. When the bond matures, you "extend the ladder" by rolling the principal into a new set of bonds. You can then sit back and enjoy your interest payments. You could start with bonds that are one year, three years, five years, and seven years, for instance.

When the first bond matures in a year, you will still have bonds with maturities of two years, four years, and six years. The recently matured bond's proceeds may be used to purchase an additional one-year bond or to roll out to a bond with a longer term, such as an eight-year bond.

Risk: A bond ladder eliminates one of the main risks associated with purchasing bonds, namely the risk that you will have to purchase a new bond when your current bond matures and interest rates may not be in your favor.

Bonds also carry additional risks. Corporate bonds are not guaranteed by the government like Treasury bonds are, so if the company defaults, you could lose your principal. Furthermore, you should own a variety of bonds to spread your risk and reduce the possibility that a single bond will negatively impact your portfolio as a whole. Your bonds' value might decrease if global interest rates increase.

Due to these worries, many investors turn to bond exchange-traded funds (ETFs), which offer a diversified fund of bonds that can be set up into a ladder, removing the possibility that one bond will negatively affect your returns.

14. social media-sponsored posts
Do you have a sizable online following on platforms like Instagram or TikTok? Obtain payment from developing consumer brands to post about their goods or otherwise highlight them in your feed.

But you'll need to keep adding engaging content to your profile to keep your audience interested. And to do that, you must keep coming up with posts that expand your audience and interact with your social media fans.

Possibility: Making use of your social media presence is a promising business strategy. With compelling content, you can attract attention and clicks to your profile. You can then monetize that content by arranging sponsored posts from companies that your followers will find interesting.

Risk: Starting here can be a Catch-22 situation because you need a big audience to get worthwhile sponsored posts, but you won't be a desirable option until you have a worthwhile audience. As a result, there is no assurance that you will be successful until you devote a significant amount of effort to expanding your audience. Spending a lot of effort creating content and keeping up with trends might lead to you receiving the sponsorship you want in the end.

Even if you start receiving the sponsored posts you want, you'll still need to keep writing to grow your following and continue to be a desirable option for advertisers. Even if you have a lot of discretion about when to do it, this calls for a larger time and financial commitment.

15. Consider opening a high-yield saving or a CD.

You can earn a passive income and receive one of the highest interest rates in the nation by opening a high-yield certificate of deposit (CD) or savings account at an online bank. Even better, earning money won't require you to leave your home.

Opportunity: To get the most out of your CD, you should quickly look up the best savings accounts or CD rates available nationwide. Going with an online bank rather than your neighborhood bank is typically much more advantageous because you'll be able to choose the best rate on offer in the nation. A guaranteed return of principal up to $250,000 is still available to you if your financial institution is FDIC-insured.

Risk: Your principal is secure as long as your bank is FDIC-backed and operates within set parameters. Thus, the safest return you can find it in a CD or savings account. Additionally, that return may be insufficient to offset inflation, which would reduce the real purchasing power of your money. But, storing your money in cash or a checking account that doesn't pay interest will result in lower returns than a CD or savings account.

16. Renting out your house temporarily

This easy method turns unused space into a source of income by utilizing space that you wouldn't otherwise use. Consider renting out your existing apartment while you're away if you're leaving town for an extended period, going on vacation, or perhaps just wishing to travel.

Opportunity: You can define your rental conditions and offer your property on any number of websites, including Airbnb. With little more labor, especially if you're renting to a renter who could stay for a few months, you can earn a check for your efforts.

Risk: There aren't many financial risks involved in this, but allowing guests into your home entails a unique kind of danger not often associated with passive investments. Your property might be damaged, destroyed, or even have assets stolen by tenants.

17. Promote on your vehicle

By merely driving your car around town, you might be able to make some additional cash. Get in touch with a professional advertising firm, and they will assess your driving patterns, including where you go and how far you travel. The agency will "wrap" your automobile with the advertisements at no expense to you if you are a good fit for one of their sponsors. Agencies like modern vehicles and drivers have to have a spotless driving record.

Opportunity: While driving is required, if you're already putting in the mileage, this is a terrific opportunity to earn hundreds of dollars each month with little to no additional expense. It is possible to pay drivers per mile.

Risk: If this idea appeals to you, take additional caution to associate with a trustworthy business. Numerous con artists set up schemes in this area to defraud you of thousands.

18. Publish a blog or a YouTube channel.

Are you an authority on Thailand travel? or a Minecraft guru? A swing-dancing sultan?

Create a blog or YouTube channel out of your enthusiasm for a subject, then monetize it with sponsors or adverts to make money. Pick a topic that is well-liked, even a little niche, and become an authority on it. You'll need to develop a content library and attract readers initially, but as you establish a reputation for your interesting content, it can eventually generate a continuous cash stream.

Possibility: You may utilize a free (or affordable) platform, then use your excellent content to get followers. Your chances of becoming "the" person to follow are stronger if your voice or area of interest is more distinctive. Draw sponsors to you then.

Risk: You'll need to start by developing content and then continue to do so, which might take time. And you'll need to be enthusiastic about the product, since it will keep you inspired to keep going, especially in the beginning when your followers are still gaining interest in you.

If there is minimal interest in your topic or niche, the actual drawback is that you may spend a lot of time and money with little to show for it. You won't know for sure unless you try, but your field of expertise may be too specialized to attract a sizable audience.

19. Rent out practical home goods

Consider starting even smaller with other home things that people might need but that might be gathering dust in your garage as an alternative to renting out an idle automobile. Lawnmowers? power equipment? Tools and a toolbox for mechanics? Large coolers or tents? Search for expensive products that individuals only occasionally require and where owning the item might not make sense. Provide a method for customers to find your merchandise and a method for them to pay for it.

Opportunity: If there is interest in a specific area, you may start small here and grow up later. As the weather changes, do people suddenly desire a tent for a weekend camping trip? Find out where there is a need for the item, and then go out and get it there rather than keeping it on hand. After a few uses, you could in certain situations be able to recover the item's worth.

Risk: There's a chance that your stuff may get destroyed or stolen, but you can reduce this risk by using contracts that let you replace the item at the client's expense. Starting modestly reduces your exposure to danger, especially if you currently own the item and aren't likely to need it very soon. Pay close attention to liability concerns, especially if you're renting out potentially harmful equipment (e.g., power tools.)

20. Provide designs online

If you are talented in design, you might be able to generate money by selling products with your printed designs. You may sell goods with your designs on sites like CafePress and Zazzle, including T-shirts, caps, mugs, and more.

Possibility: You may start with your ideas, gauge market interest, and grow from there. You might be able to take advantage of people's growing interest in a current issue and create a shirt that, at the very least, offers a sarcastic interpretation of it. Moreover, you may create your online storefront to sell your goods using a website like Shopify.

Risk: One of the major hazards of tying up your funds is avoided by using printing partners, who enable you to send products without directly investing in the product yourself. Nevertheless, if you invest in part of the goods yourself, you might be able to obtain a better deal. Another significant risk is that you may spend a lot of time on this with little return, but if you're already working on the design for another reason, like personal curiosity, this approach might be intriguing.

21. Create an annuity
A smart place to start setting up dependable income is an annuity. When you purchase a standard annuity, you pay a financial institution—usually an insurance company—money in exchange for a future income stream. Annuities are monthly payments that can be set up in several different ways, such as to begin paying immediately or long later.

Opportunity: Annuities are the epitome of passive income and may be set up in a large variety of ways based on your specific needs. The insurance company can arrange for a monthly reimbursement right away, or you can schedule the payment so that it begins, say, when you retire. Also, depending on how well the assets in the annuity performed, you might set up an annuity with a fixed return or one that may yield a variable payment.

An annuity may be set up to pay out for a certain amount of time, such as 20 years, or a lifetime. If you pass away, the payment can end, or it might keep going to your spouse. There are many choices.

Risk: Annuities are quite complicated, and once you put one up, you're sometimes locked in for a considerable amount of time. Nevertheless, you may be able to get out by paying a large penalty. You should carefully read the contract's tiny print to completely grasp the advantages and disadvantages of the particular agreement.

Every annuity contract is distinct, and each one could provide a special combination of advantages to meet your particular needs. Hence, it's crucial to comprehend what you're agreeing to.

22. Purchase a local company

You have the opportunity to create a cash flow stream through an established and operated local business. If the company is successful enough, you could even be able to pay a manager to operate it while you only participate in the most important choices, if any at all. To reduce the early danger to your own money, you might be able to purchase it with an alluring loan.

Opportunity: Local firms may have desirable and lucrative niches that you may invest in and which are difficult for rivals to imitate. In the beginning, when you become more familiar with the situation, you might be able to capitalize on the seller's qualifications or experience. A seller's willingness to finance a portion of the transaction may provide some motivation for them to see the company prosper. Moreover, you may condition a portion of the purchase price on specific profit targets or other measures.

Risk: Carefully vetting any prospective acquisition candidates is necessary to avoid purchasing a company that is far less lucrative than it seems to be or that has dwindling prospects. Working with knowledgeable and trustworthy brokers can help you get the best offer and avoid problems. You can also engage a consultant to assist you to assess possible deals. Also, if you're employing a manager to operate the store, you'll need to make sure they're trustworthy and capable else you'll run into issues.

23. Get a blog.
Consider purchasing one and bypassing the line on making one if you want to start blogging. You can obtain the previous owner's connections and associations, and you might be able to bring your own as well. Also, you don't have to wait while you create when you can start making money right away.

Chance: Purchasing a blog puts you in the game now rather than tomorrow, but you'll need to be informed and enthusiastic about it beforehand. It will be even better if you have some suggestions on how to make the blog better (better content, more effective, less expensive, etc.) so you may use it to increase profitability beyond what the purchase price may have suggested.

Risk: If you decide you want to move on to something greener, a blog, like any business, is not very liquid, so you could not get what you paid for it or even be able to sell it at all. Of course, you also need to be able to accurately assess the market and create material that readers will want to read or that will draw sponsors or other sources of income.

Which source of passive income is the best?
Which passive income source is ideal relies on several variables, but the most crucial ones are your financial situation, the size of the overall opportunity, your aptitude and interest in the sector, the time commitment required, and your chances of success. The more rivals there

are and the smaller the chance of success, generally speaking, the lower the entry barriers.

Hence, you must evaluate the possibility in light of these elements and determine which passive income approach suits you the most. Yet, it might be advantageous to possess the innate talent and a keen interest in the field you choose to pursue because these traits can serve as sources of inspiration when times are rough.

For individuals who are starting with little money as well as those who have no money at all, there are prospects for passive income.

How can I get passive income without any cash?
If you're starting with little to no money, you'll need to rely mostly on your time commitment to get you through, at least until you start saving up some money. It implies concentrating on sources of passive income that benefit from the following characteristics:

a field in which you are an authority. Here, you may leverage your skills in areas like design, software development, and others to create a meaningful good or service for customers.

a work-intensive opportunity upfront. You'll need a chance that involves putting in some time or effort, like developing a course, an influencer profile, or another choice.

In essence, until you have enough money to increase your prospects, you are replacing your time for your lack of wealth.

How can I use the money to generate passive income?

You can find additional passive investing alternatives with money. You have both the opportunity described above and a new range if you have money to invest in a passive opportunity. To benefit from the following passive income sources, you need money:

purchasing dividend-paying stocks or REITs. Although investing in stocks requires an initial financial outlay, the rewards are among the most passive income streams available.

Bonds or CDs are good ways to save. Purchasing bonds or CDs is another pure passive activity.

If that's what you'd like to do, you may utilize your money here to generate money with little to no work on your side. Of course, you may combine your cash with a significant time commitment to enter a market that is much more rewarding.

How many sources of income ought one to have?
When it comes to creating revenue streams, no advice is "one size fits all." Your financial situation and future financial goals should determine how many sources of income you have. But having a few is a fantastic place to start.

With more lines in the water, you'll catch more fish, the saying goes. "Rental properties, income-producing assets, and company initiatives are wonderful ways to diversify your revenue stream, in addition to the earned income created through your human capital."

Naturally, you'll want to make sure that working on a new passive income stream isn't taking your attention away from your current revenue sources. To ensure that you're selecting the finest chances for your time, you should balance your efforts.

Ideas for passive income for beginners

An account with a high rate of return. One simple approach to increase your savings above what you would earn in a standard checking or savings account is by opening a high-yield savings account. Although it won't be much, it's a quick method to begin earning passive money. deposit certificates. Another approach to get some passive income is through certificates of deposit (CDs), although doing so would tie up your funds more than they would in high-yield savings accounts.

trusts for investing in real estate. Real estate investment trusts (REITs) offer an easy option to invest in real estate without having to deal with the hassle of property management. REITs are a desirable alternative for investors seeking passive income since they generally distribute the bulk of their revenue in the form of dividends.

Reduce your passive income taxes

A passive income can be a terrific approach for making extra money, but you'll also incur tax obligations. Yet by establishing yourself as a company and opening a retirement account, you may lessen the tax burden while still planning for the future. But, this method won't work for all of these passive tactics, and to be eligible, your company must be legal.

Get a tax identification number for your company by registering with the IRS.
Next get in touch with a broker, who can start a retirement account for independent contractors.
Choose the retirement account type that would suit yours needs the best.
If you store the money in a regular 401(k) or SEP IRA, you may claim a tax benefit on this year's taxes. Two of the most common alternatives are the solo 401(k) and the SEP IRA. The solo 401(k) is fantastic because you may contribute up to 100% of your earnings, up to the yearly limit, to the account. The SEP IRA, however, only permits contributions at a 25 percent rate. Moreover, the solo 401(k) allows

you to contribute another contribution of up to 25% of your business revenues.

If you're considering taking this path, contrast the two account types or look at the top retirement plans for independent contractors.

CHAPTER 5:

PROTECTING YOUR WEALTH AND ASSETS

Wealth preservation is one of the key elements of any estate plan or wealth management plan in general. You must make sure that your assets are properly protected in the interim if you want to be able to pass them down to future generations. When individuals become wealthier, they also become more vulnerable to lawsuits that aim to profit from their hard-earned riches, which is why many people worry that a turbulent market climate or poor investment choice would cause them to lose a significant percentage of their assets.

Thankfully, many asset transfer strategies also offer advantages for wealth preservation. By removing your name from your assets and transferring them into legally protected structures, such as trusts or limited liability companies, thorough estate planning helps protect your family's fortune. Your money may be safeguarded by certain insurance coverage in the case of legal issues. The following tactics can assist you as you go through the estate planning process in making sure that your money isn't needlessly jeopardized while you're still alive.

1. Ownership of Assets

If you become the target of a court battle, retitling your assets can assist prevent their seizure. Although it might not be practicable or possible to retitle all of your assets, you can preserve some assets, such as a house or rental property, by removing your name from the public record.

If you're married, one approach you may apply in some jurisdictions is naming your assets as tenants-by-the-entirety with a spouse. When one spouse passes away, the asset is instantly transferred to the remaining spouse, who becomes the asset's sole owner. Additionally, if a judgment is rendered against one spouse for his or her single obligations or liabilities, the assets possessed by tenants-by-the-entirety are often shielded from creditors. In some circumstances, assets held in IRAs and eligible retirement plans (in some states) may also be safeguarded.

2. Insurance

When assets are handed to your heirs, life insurance can assist reduce estate, gift, and income taxes while giving your recipients a lump amount of money upon your passing. Moreover, additional insurance products including property, casualty, and liability insurance provide defense against a wide range of legal threats. Making sure you're adequately protected might be a wise first line of defense if your field of work tends to expose you to a lot of liability and pointless litigation.

3. Entities with Limited Liability

Establishing a limited liability company is a practical approach to keep your assets distinct from those of your company or other sources of income, such as rental property. One benefit of doing this is that responsibility for actions taken within the business is often constrained to the entity's assets. Nevertheless, if you don't divide your assets, creditors may be able to confiscate both your personal and business-related assets if a lawsuit is filed against your company, costing you everything.

4. Indestructible Trusts

If you give assets to an irrevocable trust, the trust takes ownership of those assets and you lose control over how they are dispersed. Even if you designate yourself as the beneficiary, creditors cannot access the assets to fulfill a judgment since the trust owns them. The trust's assets that have been given to beneficiaries, however, are still vulnerable to claims.

5. Trusts for asset protection

A trust for asset protection may be held onshore or offshore. It is one of the most effective strategies available to safeguard your money against creditors and is an irreversible, self-settled trust. Even though the trust may provide infrequent payouts, these distributions are only permitted at the trustee's discretion.

Domestic asset protection trusts may not be a practical option for many people as well as they are only permitted in a few states.

Wealth preservation techniques are a crucial part of your estate plan and overall wealth management strategy since your assets may be at risk for several causes that are out of your control. Whichever tactic, or combination of tactics, you decide to use, it's crucial to put it in place before any legal action is taken against you since doing so after the fact may result in a whole new set of issues. Talking about these alternatives with your financial adviser or estate planning lawyer may be a good first step in securing your family's wealth because you have a variety of options accessible to you.

Why protecting your wealth is crucial

Money matters. The possessions we have amassed or produced are essential to allowing us to live the lifestyle we choose. But, it makes sense that we would also want to protect our riches and leave as much as we can to the next generation. It's our legacy, giving us comfort in knowing we've done our part to ensure the future of our loved ones.

Wealth preservation is all about how we preserve and leave that heritage, and many various methods may assist us in doing so.

Yet talking about it isn't always simple. After all, we don't often like to think about things like death or major disease. It's complicated and emotionally charged, so it makes sense to consult a seasoned money consultant who isn't biased.

WHAT COULD I DO TO PROTECT MY WEALTH?

There are several strategies you may use to protect your fortune for future generations. A successful wealth protection strategy will frequently incorporate a variety of tactics that are specifically suited to your requirements and preferences.

life assurance

The most valuable asset in your family is likely you, but are you truly insured for your worth? A quick and easy way to provide financial support for your dependents in the event of your passing is through life insurance.

cover for serious illnesses

If you were to have a terrible disease, how would your family handle it? What would happen if you were to live yet never be able to work again? With the diagnosis of certain life-threatening or incapacitating disorders, critical illness insurance provides a tax-free lump amount. It's one technique to make a challenging situation just a little bit easier.

Income security coverage

If you are sick or hurt and are unable to work, income protection might be a lifesaver in helping you manage your finances.

draft a will

Having a current will in place is the cornerstone of successful wealth protection. You may rest easy knowing that your possessions will be distributed to the individuals you choose to inherit them should you pass away. It may help people you leave behind feel less confused and unhappy, and it may help your estate avoid paying extra taxes. Find out more about estate planning and wills here.

Choosing an attorney-in-fact
A Power of Attorney guarantees that your loved ones may carry out your desires on your behalf if you become incapacitated and unable to handle your affairs. Both money and worry can be greatly reduced.

Planning for inheritance taxes
The greatest approach to guarantee that your loved ones won't face a significant tax burden in the case of your death is via early and efficient planning. Your legacy may be significantly impacted by inheritance tax. Your money advisor will be able to provide you with some suggestions on how to prevent it from happening.

trust management
Although trusts are a difficult area of planning, they may simply make sure that the proper

amount of money is distributed to the right individuals at the right time.

protection of property
You could eventually require treatment. Your assets may be severely depleted by the costs of residential care, and in many situations, you may need to sell your family home to get the necessary funds.

Property protection examines how you might alter the ownership of your house to safeguard your partner and/or beneficiaries.

WHY IS PROTECTING WEALTH SO IMPORTANT?
If the wrong safeguards are not in place, the results might be disastrous. None of us have any idea what is in store. Years may be spent creating the money that allows us to live happily and comfortably, control our destinies, and secure the futures of others we care about. But, that sense of security and tranquility may be abruptly taken away by death or a catastrophic disease.

Your family will be safeguarded from any unforeseen situations thanks to an efficient wealth protection plan. That gives both you and their comfort.

Please don't hesitate to contact us if you have any questions about how to protect your investments; one of our knowledgeable wealth managers will be pleased to assist you.

Tax rates, bases, and exemptions are all subject to change at any time. Any tax relief's worth is based on the circumstances of the individual.

Powers of Attorney and will be writing need a referral to a service that is unique from those provided by St. James's Place. The Financial Conduct Authority does not regulate wills or powers of attorney.

Understanding different types of insurance

Although we can't always stop the unexpected from happening, there are occasions when we can shield our families and ourselves from the worst financial consequences.

Based on your unique circumstances, including those related to children, age, lifestyle, and work perks, you should choose the appropriate type and amount of insurance.

The majority of financial professionals advise purchasing life, health, vehicle, and long-term disability insurance.

Insurance Types Everyone Needs

1. Health Insurance
Traditional whole life and term life are the two fundamental forms of life insurance.

As an income source and an insurance mechanism, the whole life can be employed. Both a death benefit and a cash value component are included. You may access the money as the value increases by taking out a loan or a withdrawal, and you can cancel the insurance by accepting the cash value.

With term life insurance, your coverage lasts for a predetermined period, such as 10, 20, or 30, and your premiums are constant. A term policy, which is typically the least expensive kind of life insurance, can be used to cover the years that a mortgage loan is in default or the duration of your children's college careers.

If your family depends on your income, life insurance is extremely crucial. Experts in the field advise purchasing a policy that pays out 10 times your annual income.

Include funeral costs when calculating the amount of life insurance you require. Then determine the cost of everyday living for your household. Mortgage payments, unpaid debts, credit card debt, taxes, childcare expenses, and upcoming education expenses are a few examples.

More than half of U.S. households depend on multiple incomes, according to a 2021 research by LIMRA, previously known as the Life Insurance and Market Research Association. The survey also discovered that 25% of households would face financial difficulty within a month of losing a wage earner.

2. Medical Insurance
Health insurance can be purchased privately for yourself and your family by contacting health insurance companies directly or going through a health insurance agent, as well as via your employer, the federal health insurance marketplace, or other sources.

According to the Centers for Disease Control's (CDC) National Center for Health Statistics, just 9.2% of Americans did not have health insurance in 2021. The other 40% were covered by government-funded programs including Medicare and Medicaid, veterans' benefits programs, and the federal marketplace created by the Affordable Care Act, while more than 60% obtained their coverage through their employment or the private insurance market.

Even a small coverage is preferable to none if your finances are tight. One of the 80 million Americans who qualify for Medicaid may be you if your income is modest.

You can qualify for subsidized coverage under the federal Affordable Care Act if your income is moderate yet doesn't allow you to afford insurance coverage.

If your workplace offers insurance, signing up for it is typically the best and least expensive choice for salaried workers. According to research by the Kaiser Family Foundation, the average annual premium cost to the employee in an employer-sponsored healthcare program in 2021 was $7,739 for single coverage and $22,221 for a family plan.

3. Covering for Long-Term Disability
Those who become unable to work are supported by long-term disability insurance. One in four people who begin the workforce will become incapacitated before they reach retirement age, according to the Social Security Administration.

While hospitalization and medical expenditures are covered by health insurance, you are frequently responsible for all the costs that your salary would have paid. Both short-term and long-term disability insurance is frequently provided by businesses as a part of their benefits package. This would be the most advantageous strategy for obtaining inexpensive disability insurance.

Here are some things to think about before buying insurance on your own if your company doesn't provide long-term coverage:

The best course of action is to ensure income replacement. Several insurance plans cover 40% to 70% of your salary.

Age, way of life, and health are just a few of the numerous variables that affect how much disability insurance will cost. The typical cost is from 1% to 3% of your yearly pay.

Read the small print before making a purchase. Many policies contain severe policy exclusions, a three-month waiting period before coverage begins, and a three-year maximum length of coverage.

4. Vehicle Insurance

The National Highway Traffic Safety Administration estimates that in the first nine months of 2021, 31,720 persons died in traffic accidents on U.S. roads and highways, despite years of advancements in automobile safety.

The few jurisdictions that don't need auto insurance nonetheless hold drivers financially liable for any damage or injuries they cause. Nearly all states mandate that drivers have auto insurance. You have the following choices when buying auto insurance:

If you cause an accident and are found at fault, liability coverage will pay for any property damage and personal injuries you cause to other people. It will also pay for any legal fees and judgments or settlements if you are sued as a result of the accident.

Collision and comprehensive insurance: Regardless of who was at blame for the incident, collision insurance will pay to repair or replace your automobile. Theft and damage to your automobile resulting from flooding, hail, fire, vandalism, fallen items, and animal strikes are all covered by comprehensive insurance. This kind of insurance is required when you lease or loan a vehicle.

Uninsured/underinsured motorist (UM) coverage: If an uninsured or underinsured driver impacts your car, this insurance covers your medical bills and those of your passenger, as well as potentially lost wages and pain and suffering damages.

Personal injury protection (PIP): PIP insurance helps cover the expenses of medical treatment and missed income for you and your passengers.

Medical payment coverage (MedPay): If you are hurt in an accident, MedPay coverage can assist cover your medical costs, which are normally between $1,000 and $5,000 for you and your passengers.

Like with any insurance, the price will depend on your specific situation. Check often to see whether you qualify for a reduced rate depending on your age, driving history, or the region where you reside. Compare various rate estimates and the coverage offered.

The vast majority of experts concur that you absolutely must obtain life, health, long-term disability, and car insurance. Employer coverage is frequently the best choice, but if that is not a possibility, get prices from many companies because many of them provide savings if you buy multiple types of coverage.

CHAPTER 6:

MASTERING YOUR MONEY HABITS

For many people, achieving financial freedom—having enough cash on hand, investments, and savings to support the lifestyle they choose for themselves and their families—is a top priority. Developing a nest egg that would enable you to retire or follow whatever job you like also means removing the pressure of having to make a particular amount of money each year.

Regrettably, far too many people lack financial independence. Even in the absence of sporadic financial problems, the continual load of mounting debt brought on by excessive spending prevents them from achieving their objectives. Further gaps in safety nets are exposed when a severe crisis—like a storm, an earthquake, or a pandemic—destroys all arrangements.

Nearly everyone has trouble, but by adopting these behaviors, you may steer clear of it.

Being financially self-sufficient
Financial independence is the ability to live comfortably for the rest of one's life and fulfill all of one's commitments without depending on a wage. The ultimate objective of a long-term financial strategy is that.

1. Choose Your Life's Objectives
How do you define financial independence? Everyone wants it in general, but that's a very nebulous objective. You must be precise about sums and due dates. The possibility of completing your goals increases with their level of specificity.

Put these three goals in writing:

What is needed for your lifestyle
How much cash do you need to have in your account to make it happen
What age is the cutoff for saving that much?
Establish financial mileposts at regular intervals between the two dates as you work

your way backward from your deadline age to your present age. Put the target sheet at the front of your financial binder and be sure to write down all amounts and deadlines precisely.

2. Establish a monthly budget.
The easiest method to ensure that all bills are paid and savings are progressing as planned is to create a monthly household budget and adhere to it. Also, having a schedule helps you stay committed to your objectives and resist the inclination to indulge.

3. Repay all of your credit card debt
The process of accumulating money is poisoned by high-interest consumer loans and credit cards. Make it a point to settle the bill in full each month. Paying off student debts, mortgages, and other comparable loans is not urgent because their interest rates are often significantly lower. Even yet, timely repayment of these loans with reduced interest rates is crucial since it improves credit standing.

4. Automatically save money

First, pay yourself. Participate in the retirement program offered by your workplace, and make use of any matching contribution benefits—free money—to the fullest. It's a good idea to set up automatic contributions to a brokerage account or a similar account, as well as withdrawals into an emergency fund that may be used for unforeseen needs.

The money for your emergency fund and retirement account should ideally be taken out of your account the same day you were paid, so it never even comes into contact with your hands.

Bear in mind that your specific situation will determine how much money is advised to be saved in an emergency fund. Also, you shouldn't use a tax-advantaged retirement plan as your sole source of emergency funds because of the limitations that make it challenging to get your funds if you unexpectedly need them.

5. Now is the time to invest

Many may doubt the idea of investing during bad markets, but historically there has never been a better chance to increase your wealth. Your money will expand tremendously thanks to the magic of compound interest alone, but you'll need a lot of time to see real growth.

But, keep in mind that doing the type of stock selection made popular by billionaires like Warren Buffett would be a mistake for anybody other than experienced investors. Instead, register an online brokerage account that enables you to easily learn how to invest, build a modest portfolio, and automatically add funds to it every week or month. To assist you in getting started, we've listed the top online brokers for beginners.

In the face of mounting debt, cash crises, medical expenses, and excessive spending, achieving financial independence can be quite challenging. Yet, it is attainable with discipline and careful preparation. The ultimate objective of

6. Be aware of your credit score
Your credit score is a crucial factor in determining the interest rate you are given

whether purchasing a home or a new automobile.

It also affects how much you spend on a variety of other necessities, such as life insurance premiums and auto insurance.

Because someone with hazardous financial habits is thought to be likely to also be reckless in other aspects of life, such as not taking care of their health—or even driving and drinking—credit ratings are given a lot of weight.

This is why it's crucial to obtain a copy of your credit report frequently to ensure that no inaccurate negative information is tarnishing your reputation. To further secure your information, it would be worthwhile to investigate a trustworthy credit monitoring service.

7. bargain for products and services

For fear of coming out as cheap, many Americans are reluctant to haggle for products and services. By overcoming this fear, you might annually save thousands of lives. Bulk purchases or presenting yourself as a loyal client might get you substantial discounts since small firms, in particular, frequently engage in negotiating.

8. Maintain Your Financial Education

To make sure that all adjustments and deductions are maximized each year, review pertinent changes in tax legislation. Follow market changes and financial news, and don't be afraid to rebalance your investment portfolio as necessary. The strongest safeguard against scammers who rely on inexperienced investors to make a fast profit is knowledge.

9. Upkeep of Your Property

Everything from vehicles and lawnmowers to shoes and clothing lasts longer when the property is well-maintained. Maintenance is an investment that should not be overlooked because it is far less expensive than replacement.

Learn to distinguish between what you desire and what you need.

10. Living within your means
A mindset centered on making the most of less is necessary for mastering a thrifty way of life, and it's simpler than you would think. In reality, many successful people formed the practice of living within their means before becoming affluent.

Adopting a simple lifestyle is not difficult. It simply entails developing the ability to tell the difference between goods you need and things you desire and then making modest changes that result in significant improvements to your financial well-being.

11. Make use of a financial advisor
Get a financial counselor to help you continue on the correct track once you've accumulated a respectable amount of money, either in liquid assets (cash or anything that can be changed into cash) or fixed assets (property or anything that cannot be converted into cash).

12. Maintain Your Health
Taking exceptional care of your physical health has a major beneficial influence on your

financial health as well. The notion of regular maintenance also applies to your body.

It is simple to invest in your health. It entails going to the dentist and doctor regularly and adhering to medical recommendations for any issues you experience. Simple lifestyle adjustments, including increasing exercise and eating better, can help—or even prevent—many medical conditions.

On the other hand, poor health maintenance has adverse short- and long-term effects on your financial objectives. Because some employers only allow a certain number of paid sick days, once those days are used up, money is lost. In addition to forcing early retirement with a lesser monthly income for the rest of your life, poor health can cause insurance costs to increase and cause obesity and other dietary disorders.

Financial freedom: What Is It?
Everyone has their definition of financial independence. For the majority of individuals, this is having enough money (in the form of

savings, investments, and cash) to support a particular standard of living, as well as a nest egg for retirement or the flexibility to choose any line of work without regard to compensation.

What Is the Budget Rule of 50/30/20?
The 50/30/20 budget rule, made popular by Senator Elizabeth Warren, proposes splitting after-tax income into three areas of spending: necessities (50%) and desires (30%); and savings and debt repayment (20%). To assist you in categorizing and controlling your spending and saving—the crucial first step toward financial freedom—we have created an intuitive budgeting calculator.

Would My Car Insurance Increase If I Have a Low Credit Score?
Several firms utilize a credit-based scoring system to evaluate whether to insure you and how much you will pay, even though certain states—including California, Hawaii, Washington, Massachusetts, and Michigan—limit or forbid the use of credit scores to calculate vehicle insurance prices.

Although these methods won't fix all of your financial issues, they will assist you in creating positive habits that will put you on the road to financial security. Merely creating a plan with precise dollar amounts and due dates strengthens your desire to accomplish your objective and protects you against the need to overspend. Financial independence is within reach once you begin to make actual progress and are freed from the continual strain of mounting debt. These two factors also act as potent motivators.

The role of habits in building wealth

Setting up a few wise habits can help you master your finances.

After all, according to Thomas C. Corley, who conducted extensive research on hundreds of self-made millionaires for his book "Change Your Habits, Change Your Life," "habits are the cause of wealth, poverty, happiness, sadness, stress, good relationships, bad relationships, good health, or bad health."

Simple financial practices you can start today

1. Automate your money management.

According to self-made millionaire David Bach, you should immediately put your financial plan on auto-pilot if it isn't already. You can easily accumulate wealth by automating your finances by transferring your money to creditors, savings accounts, and investment accounts regularly.

According to Bach in "The Automatic Millionaire," it's "the one step that virtually guarantees that you won't fail financially." You won't ever forget a payment again, and you won't ever be tempted to cut back on savings because you won't even see the money going from your paycheck to your savings accounts.

Simply link your accounts, designate the precise day you want to make transfers, and money will be transferred directly from your paycheck to your 401(k) or from your checking account to your savings account.

Automation "frees up valuable time and allows you to focus on the fun parts of life, rather than spend time worrying about whether you paid that bill or if you're going to overdraft again," according to Bach. Automation also ensures that you never make a late payment again.

2. Put your "spare change" to use.

Contrary to popular belief, investing doesn't require a lot of capital to get started, making it one of the most efficient ways to accumulate wealth.

You can start by simply investing your "spare change" thanks to micro-investing apps like Acorns, which will automatically round up your purchases to the nearest dollar and put any spare change to work.

Additionally, automated investing services known as robo-advisors can work for you regardless of how much money you have in the bank, and other apps also aim to make investing easy and accessible.

The main lesson to be learned is to start investing as soon as possible to fully benefit from compound interest. According to Bach, "the miracle of compounding can turn a relatively modest but dependable amount of saving into significant wealth."

3. Give up making petty, routine purchases like your morning coffee.

Bach created the phrase "The Latte Factor," which proposes that giving up your $5 daily latte could enable you to save a significant sum of money over time.

You can use this money in the same way that you can use your spare change. The cost of a $5 daily coffee is roughly $35 per week or $150 per month. According to Bach, if you put $150 away each month and earned a 10% annual return, you would have $948,611 at the end of 40 years.

We all waste too much of our hard-earned money on unnecessary "little" expenses without realizing how much they can add up to, the financial advisor advises. Start by figuring out your "latte factor," cut back on that expense, and direct the money towards an investment account.

4. Set up specific financial objectives.

Rich people are completely clear about their desire for wealth, which is the main reason why most people don't get what they want.

He advises setting goals for your annual income and net worth to achieve that level of clarity. Be realistic when setting goals, but don't be afraid to push yourself. After all, the richest individuals aren't afraid to have big ideas.

5. Spending unplanned money should be avoided.

Pretend that additional funds, such as a bonus, a check for your birthday, or any other windfall, don't exist.

Develop the habit of using any unexpected money, even a $20 bill you found in your coat pocket. Use it for your emergency fund, debt, student loans, or investment account. That will total up. Also, developing this practice early on can aid you in preventing lifestyle inflation should you receive an unexpected increase in income.

6. Remind yourself that you deserve wealth.

The self-made millionaire Steve Siebold writes in his book "How Rich People Think" that the greatest people have a single belief that "success, fulfillment, and happiness are the natural order of existence," and that this belief "drives the great ones to behave in ways that virtually guarantee their success."

The self-made billionaire says that on the other hand, the typical earner stays ordinary because they anticipate being so: "The majority think they aren't deserving of tremendous fortune. They ponder, "Who am I to become a millionaire?" "

Try pondering the question, "Why not me?

That's what millionaires and billionaires do, after all.

7. Read for 30 minutes each day.

People with money like to read. Long after their official education is complete, they continue to teach and invest in themselves. One of the first things you'll notice when you enter a wealthy person's home is their extensive library of self-help books, according to the saying, "Walk into a wealthy person's home and you'll see,"

You might succeed if it works for millionaires and billionaires.

8. Your alarm should be sooner.

Apart from reading, rich individuals often rise early. Self-made millionaires Jack Dorsey and Richard Branson wake up at five in the morning to begin their days, but they are hardly the only prosperous individuals who rise early.

I discovered that over 50% of the self-made billionaires I studied over five years got up at least three hours before their workday started.

Although we cannot promise that becoming a member of the early bird club will make you wealthy, it can't harm you and will almost surely increase your productivity.

9. Be in the company of wealthy, successful people.

It's more important than you might think who you hang out with. In actuality, your wealth often reflects that of your closest friends.

The self-made millionaire writes, "Successful people generally agree that consciousness is contagious and that exposure to more successful people has the potential to expand your thinking and catapult your income." "Because we emulate those we surround ourselves with, success attracts success,"

In search of a fresh group to roll with? "If there's no way you can afford to join a high-end club, have coffee or tea in the classiest hotel in your city," he writes. "Consider joining a high-end tennis, golf, health, or business club." Get comfortable in this setting and observe the customers, noting that they are just like you.

10. Maintain a spending log.

If more money is going out of your pocket than is entering, you cannot increase your wealth. Track your everyday costs to make sure you're bringing in more money than you're spending.

There are a few apps that can help you with this, including Level Money, Personal Capital, and Mint. You can simply keep track of your regular purchases in a notebook or on your phone, or you can use a spreadsheet on your computer.

Maybe you'll discover another "latte factor" that you can reduce.

11. Give high-interest debt a top priority.

It's critical to realize that not all debt is created equal. Ranking all of your debt from highest to lowest in terms of interest rate is a good strategy. Then, to pay less throughout your loans, prioritize the debt with the highest interest rate while continuing to make the minimum payment on all of your debts.

Another choice is to rank your debts according to size, starting with the smallest. The idea behind this method, which personal finance experts refer to as the "snowball method," is that by paying off one type of debt at a time, you gain momentum that will help you take on the next biggest one, and so on.

You must exit the red zone as soon as possible. After all, starting to accumulate wealth is challenging if you have debt.

Strategies for developing positive money habits

Particularly poor financial habits, old habits die hard. It's time to stop your poor spending habits and begin developing healthier financial ones if you realize that you have no savings and spend more than you make.

Developing wise financial practices may boost your wealth and position you for financial success. You'll gain knowledge on how to set up a budget, save money, and work toward your financial objectives.

Of course, changing negative habits and forming new ones takes time. Yet, you may begin the move to improved money habits if you are persistent and knowledgeable.

Why poor financial practices set you up for failure

It's critical to break negative financial habits as soon as you can. Poor financial habits might make you less likely to succeed and hinder you from achieving your financial objectives.

Living paycheck to paycheck, not saving money, and having bad spending habits might make you vulnerable to unforeseen situations and prevent you from having enough money for retirement. As you can see, poor money management practices may ruin your financial prospects.

bad financial habits to break
Do you know what your terrible financial habits are? Check out these money-wasting behaviors to break right now and start managing your finances responsibly!

accumulating credit card debt
Oh, those enchanted plastic cards that make it so simple to purchase the designer handbag you've been lusting for. One of the most expensive poor money habits you can have is racking up credit card debt.

Are you one of the typical Americans who owe more than $6,000 on their credit cards? You might pay hundreds to thousands of dollars in interest on high-interest credit cards.

Also, carrying large credit card debt might lower your credit score. Pay your debt in full each month to avoid wasting money on interest. You will save a ton of money and avoid debt by doing this.

When you're bored, go shopping
Shopping late at night when you're half asleep and bored was once characterized as the "home shopping network syndrome." To order these gorgeous trinkets or whatever your weakness was, you would make a call.

Online buying makes it far too simple to indulge in purchasing while bored. Boredom shopping is a dreadful financial habit that, if you're not careful, may lead to debt accumulation. Instead of buying, try these worthwhile activities.

Impulsive buying
It isn't only by accident all those delightfully placed goods are in the checkout queue. This is a sales technique used to get you to make larger purchases before you leave the store. Impulsive expenditures can swiftly drain your bank account since they pile up so quickly.

If you make $100 in impulsive purchases each month, it comes to $1200 every year. Find out how to quit shopping to break this harmful habit once and for all.

purchasing status
Do you make purchases to impress others? It might be simple to be sucked into celebrity culture and the desire to impress others with your possessions.

Shopping for status, however, is a bad method to make true friends and can ruin your finances. Keep in mind that you should always be true to yourself and that you don't need to impress others with your possessions.

Building good financial habits
Check out these 15 financial behaviors to start right away today after deciding which money habits to giving up.

1. Establish a budget
Setting up a budget is among the first wise financial practices to adopt. You may properly manage your finances with the use of a budget. By setting up a budget, you may avoid financial

pitfalls, pay your expenses on time, and amass money via savings.

You may design your budget using several different tools and techniques. Selecting the budgeting strategy that works best for you is the key to conquering budgeting obstacles.

2. Living within your means

Living within your means is one of the most beneficial financial habits you can form. Your savings account can grow quickly if you live within your means. You can also learn to distinguish between your requirements and wants to avoid developing unhealthy spending habits.

Although leading a modest lifestyle may seem difficult, you'd be astonished at how much money you can save by making even little lifestyle changes.

Small adjustments to your spending patterns, such as using coupons, buying used items rather than new ones, and cutting the cable, can have a significant influence on your bank account.

3. remit debt

Paying off your debt is one of the most crucial things you should do while creating healthy financial habits. Debt not only costs a lot of money, but it also hurts our emotions.

Although being in debt may make you feel as though you are at sea without a life raft, you may escape it with the correct debt repayment plan. You may start saving more money and safeguard your financial future by paying off your debt.

4. Automate your money.

By automating your accounts, you can make life a little easier while making sure your payments are paid on time. It is possible to set up automated bill payments and even money transfers to your savings accounts. This is a terrific approach to taking charge of your money, but you still need to routinely evaluate your accounts.

5. Create an emergency fund.

One of the worst emotions in the world is not having enough money to cover emergencies like a broken-down car, house repairs, or an unexpected job loss. One of the smartest financial decisions you can make is to increase your emergency fund.

A three to six-month supply of basic living expenditures should be set up to meet unforeseen circumstances. Feeling overwhelmed by how much you need? You might begin by setting aside $1,000 and increase from there.

6. Increase your wealth by investing

You must begin investing if you want your money to increase and become truly wealthy. Your income might go up and your financial future can be more secure if you invest your money.

To begin investing, you don't need a lot of cash. Our book, "Grow Your Money, Understand How Investing Works," will teach you all you need to know about investing.

7. obtain appropriate insurance

Being underinsured might result in significant out-of-pocket expenses. Your income and possessions can be protected by purchasing the correct insurance.

The kind of insurance coverage you require depends on your circumstances. Look out for these 9 insurance types that you might not have but that you need.

8. Go through your bank statements.

Reviewing your bank statements might help you immediately identify unlawful activities because bank account fraud is widespread.

A vigilant watch on your finances helps you identify your spending patterns and ensures that nothing slips through. Make checking your bank statements once a month a routine in your financial life.

9. Make more deductions

Try to boost your deductions as much as you can if you have a 401k. This will lower your taxable income and help you swiftly accumulate retirement savings.

Make it a point to raise your deductions to the highest amount that your company will match—doing so will be like receiving free money right in your pocket!

10. Monitor your spending
Even though you might not be writing checks anymore, it's still important to keep track of your costs. Balancing a checkbook may seem like a thing of the past.

You can stay on top of your finances and avoid financial blunders like overdrafts by keeping a spending log or diary.

11. Self-reward initially
Paying yourself first is a fantastic strategy to save money quickly. This implies that you pay yourself first by conserving cash before you spend any.

For instance, you may save a certain amount or percentage of your income each pay period. You may save money this way and spend it later. You should cultivate this money habit since you are prioritizing your financial objectives.

12. Early bill payment
It's simple to make mistakes and occasionally pay bills late, but these costs pile up and are a waste of money. Pay your bills ahead of time, not on the due day, as a favor to yourself. By doing this, you'll avoid forgetting and accruing late fines. Aim to pay a bill as soon as you get it.

13. Plan your finances.
You need to know your destination to arrive there. The same holds for your future financial situation. You may lay out your goals and take action to accomplish them with the aid of a financial plan. To help you reach your objectives faster, include both short- and long-term financial targets in your strategy.

Saving money for a trip, for instance, would be a short-term objective, while paying off your house would be a long-term one. To make achieving your long-term goals simpler, divide them into smaller objectives.

14. Limit spending

So to speak, it's time to cut the fat. You may save a ton of money each month by eliminating unneeded spending. Stop overpaying, cancel subscriptions, get rid of TV, and lower your power cost. By eliminating tiny costs, you might free up money for something you desire, like a trip. Even small expenses build up over time.

15. Be an astute consumer.

Did you know that shopping used can help you save up to 40% off retail prices? Used gadgets, jewelry, and apparel may help you save hundreds to thousands of dollars annually.

Shop at shops' discounts and clearance racks to reduce costs, and don't forget to utilize coupons and cash-back applications to further your savings!

Start a budgeting challenge today.
It might be challenging to find the motivation to stop negative behaviors and adopt positive

ones. Making something enjoyable, on the other hand, might help you relax and stay committed.

Take part in a savings challenge to start developing sound financial practices. A savings challenge is entertaining and may quickly increase the size of your bank account.

Good financial habits are the key to financial success.
You set yourself up for financial success when you adopt solid money management practices. You may achieve the financial independence you seek by making financial plans for the future, saving money, and maintaining financial discipline.

Also, you'll have money saved up for a beautiful retirement, be ready for unforeseen costs, and avoid fines and late fees.

As you develop sound financial practices, you'll notice your bank account expanding and how it will help you achieve financial success.

Giving up bad spending habits may take some getting used to, but doing so is crucial for financial freedom.

overcoming typical obstacles and difficulties

Your mentality determines whether or not you succeed.

One important characteristic that makes all the difference, in my experience working with women who want to advance in their careers and experience more joy in life, is your mindset. "Whether you think you can or think you can't — you're right," as Henry Ford famously remarked.

Organizations like schools and workplaces now operate differently thanks to the field of mindset, which was established by Stanford professor Carol Dweck. Dweck has found through her research that the mindset you adopt can significantly affect how you live your life. I've discovered that when I'm in my comfort zone, nothing great happens. My greatest successes and deepest joys come when I push myself a little, aim higher, take calculated risks, and risk failure (and, yes, maybe even succeed!).

Yes, taking chances and "failing" isn't enjoyable. But I can view my "failures" as learning opportunities if I reframe them as chances for improvement. Growing their mindset is their secret weapon, as many great leaders will tell you!

Developing a Growth Mindset is Possible
Have you ever been hesitant to try something because you were worried you wouldn't succeed? Do you decline new assignments because you lack the assurance to complete them? Are your tendencies toward perfectionism preventing you from taking on a challenging project? Wouldn't it be nice to get criticism without getting defensive and self-conscious? According to Dweck's research, those who persevere through failure tend to be happier and more successful than those who give up when difficulties arise.

In the late 1950s, when Dweck was in the sixth grade, she first became interested in mindset.

She noticed that teachers seated the students according to their IQs. Then, the students with the highest IQs were chosen to wipe the board, carry the flag, or deliver a note to the principal. She mentioned that highly gifted children were identified early on and that their achievements were consistently celebrated. But it got her thinking: Might the kids who didn't have high IQs still succeed? She began decades of research after questioning if high exam scores were connected with success. Her goal was to find out whether one's thinking affected outcomes.

Let's examine two fictitious people, Taylor and Reilly. They both work for a rapidly expanding IT business on the same team. Their employer has given them the task of coming up with fresh marketing plans for the approaching product launch. Since Taylor depends on statistics to make judgments, Taylor immediately sets to work, taking satisfaction in "doing it right." Taylor spends a few months gathering information and creating reports. Taylor doesn't want to fail and thinks there is only one successful launch approach. Taylor develops a strategy meticulously, seldom seeking input from others for fear that the ideas could be rejected or contested. Taylor wants to appear intelligent. Taylor formulates a solitary, thoroughly studied answer and will vehemently support it in a meeting.

Reilly takes a different approach to this practice. Reilly enjoys coming up with ideas and is not afraid to take chances. After conducting some research, Reilly quickly develops a few ideas that are tested in the marketplace. Some are successful while others are not. In the months that follow, Reilly continues to improve his methods after learning from his mistakes. Reilly constantly seeks out criticism and implements it into his plans.

Can you determine who offered the winning strategy to their supervisor when it was time to make a presentation? Can you guess who was then given a promotion? Who loved their work better, do you think you can guess? Certainly, Reilly's strategy fostered more innovation, individual growth, and commercial success.

Reilly showed a development mentality in his performance.

Which Mindset Do You Possess: A Fixed or a Development Mindset?

Individuals may be positioned on a continuum depending on how they see the origins of ability, claims Dweck. Do you think that success results from natural talent or through work? is the main query. You are considered to have a "fixed" theory of intellect or a fixed mentality if you think it's talent. Individuals with a "growth" mindset are those who think that perseverance, learning, and hard effort are the keys to success.

How you respond to "failure" is particularly important because those with a fixed mindset, like Taylor in the story, dread it because it is a derogatory statement about their fundamental abilities. Because they are aware that they can perform better and view failure as a valuable learning opportunity, people with growth mindsets, like Reilly, don't mind failure as much.

These two attitudes are crucial in ALL areas of your life, from business to parenting to finding personal fulfillment. According to Dweck, adopting a growth mindset can help you lead a less stressful and more fruitful life. To further her studies on the capacity to learn, Dweck received the $3.8 million Yidan Prize for Education Research in 2017, which recognized the significance of this drive to discover a workaround.

A growth mindset is a core belief that you can alter your course, evolve through time, and improve your circumstances. As a result, you will have a far wider range of alternatives to select from. You think that you are the center of control. You don't hold people accountable for your predicament or failures. You think you're in charge and can decide how things will turn out. You think that if you work hard enough, you can develop, enrich your life, and have a greater positive influence on the world around you. A fixed worldview prioritizes proving things. In a growth mentality, the goal is to advance. Do you understand why having a development mentality is so powerful?

What Mentality Do You Have In Your Organization?

It's essential to remember that companies also have attitudes. A corporation embraces and promotes a growth mentality when it promotes taking risks and celebrating failure. Employee engagement is extremely strong and innovation is prevalent in these firms. People have a high level of organizational loyalty and frequently remain. People are hesitant to attempt new things, to innovate, and to suggest improvements in fixed-mindset companies, or even in those that Talk about a growth mindset but punish risk-taking and failure. This is because they fear that if they fail, they will personally suffer consequences.

Even worse, people who work in companies with entrenched mindsets frequently lie, take shortcuts, and cheat to advance. She discovered that employees in companies with growth mindsets are 47% more likely to view their coworkers as reliable, 34% more likely to feel a strong sense of ownership and commitment to the business, 65% more likely to say that the company encourages risk-taking, and 49% more likely to say that the company fosters innovation.

Another influencing organizational mentality is reward schemes. Consider employee rewards and what happens when calculated risks go wrong. Astro Teller is the organization's leader at X, Alphabet's moonshot factory, and he openly celebrates mistakes. "Your business must regularly and publicly reward people whose initiatives fail if you want an innovative culture."

Obstacles to Having a Development Mindset
I recently finished delivering a growth mindset course online for Udemy, an online learning platform, and in it, I talk about the six barriers I see preventing individuals from embracing a growth mindset. Lack of confidence, fear of failure, fear of success, perfectionism, lethargy, and a general sense of being trapped are the six barriers mentioned above. Impostor syndrome, the perception that you are a fraud unworthy of achievement, supports both a lack of confidence and a dread of failure. You have the impression

that it's just a matter of time until others realize it! The majority of us face at least one of these obstacles, and some people face all six! The good news is that there are tried-and-true methods for getting around each obstacle.

You can get rid of your obstacles.
Self-awareness is the first step in many ways for getting rid of these obstacles. I frequently request that the individuals I coach begin by keeping a notebook. Start by writing down your barrier, then ask yourself WHY you feel this way. This is one of my favorite approaches. For instance, when I think about a discussion I have coming up, I could feel queasy. I may answer that I worry about what other people would think of me when I reflect on why. If you ask me why once more, I would respond that I desire to respect you and that people might not like the way I say things. When a third person is asked why, I can respond that I desire their respect because it will make my message more powerful. By the time I reach my fifth why, I might realize that what I fear is losing my audience's attention and my message. It turns out that this is the main reason for my fear, so I

can now deal with the real problem. My efforts will be directed toward making my message memorable and my request to the audience crystal clear. By doing this, I manage to overcome a lot of my fears related to public speaking because I stopped worrying about what the audience will think of me. I've put my message above all else and let go of my ego in the process.

At each obstacle, try one of the following specific solutions:

Lack of assurance
It's crucial to deal with the demons in your brain. How do you talk to yourself? Can the script be changed? Reframe your negative self-talk about not being good enough as a positive. Consider including the word yet. I'm still not a very good presenter. Or adopt a fresh, upbeat tone. Toggle "Am I? from "I AM! "I am competent enough. I can accomplish this. Alternatively, even if I don't execute it correctly, I'll still learn from it. Perhaps I want to embark on this journey. Thank you for choosing a constructive position. Saying "I am a confident,

compassionate and competent leader" will help you develop your intrinsic leadership talents, even if you have to "fake it 'til you make it." I once worried about presenting a keynote, so on the hour-long trip to the venue, I stuck a sticky note that read, "HAVE FUN! This small lesson reaffirmed that I don't have to be flawless and that I will probably be most effective at communicating my message by being at ease and engaging with the audience.

Anxiety of failing

Try redefining failure and even enjoying it. I have not failed, as Thomas Edison famously remarked. Oprah believes that failure is a stepping stone to success, saying, "I've just found 10,000 methods that won't work." If you had fun while doing it, it wasn't a failure. Did you truly fail, in my opinion, if you gained something? The "failure bow," which seems absurd but is a therapeutic way to accept that an approach didn't work and even have a little fun about it, is how aspiring performers celebrate failure in improv theater. In the quiet of my bedroom, right before I go to sleep, I often take the failed bow. It's a way for me to admit that although I attempted something new, this time it didn't work out. It enables me to be kinder to myself.

phobia of success

Although it seems contradictory, fear of success exists. We unintentionally hinder our progress because we worry about how things will change if we are successful. It may seem like indecision or insecurity. This is a common quality in entertainers, musicians, and athletes. They desire achievement but are apprehensive about how their lives may alter as a result. When you experiment and fail, you fall back on what you already know. You go back to where you feel at ease. If you manage to master this novel endeavor, you will be venturing into unexplored terrain. It may be unsettling and frightening. In the end, being quiet is simpler. Journaling is a terrific method to connect with inner emotions, especially ones that may have been created from early childhood events if you fear achievement. Write on what true success entails. Is the image seen here accurate? Is achievement, for instance, met with a standing ovation? having 100,000 fans? It could be beneficial to redefine success. What exactly about success makes me uneasy? What's preventing me from going for what I want? Exists anyone who could support me in my journey? What's the worst that may happen, you ask?

Perfectionism

Women appear to struggle with this quality rather frequently. They take great delight in going above and above. Yet it's crucial to consider how this feature is benefiting you. What are you NOT doing because you spend so much time making everything perfect, or how is perfectionism holding you back? Perfectionists frequently avoid taking chances because they are so frightened of failing and being less than flawless. If this is you, try posing the question, "What could possibly go wrong?" Really, how horrible is it? The best-case scenario may present a big career or life opportunity, and chances are you could gather the strength and resources to handle the worst case! Think about how your tendency for perfection may be affecting your colleagues. The best-selling author Liz Wiseman calls perfectionism a depleting quality to others around you in her book Multipliers. Others frequently give up or quit trying because they believe their efforts are never good enough. With my meticulous mother, I most definitely had this experience in the kitchen. Because Mom was constantly having to redo my work, nothing I did was ever correct or good enough, which is probably why I don't love cooking anymore. This might cause irritation and a lack of creativity on the part of your team at work (and in life). Do you want this?

Unable to Move

Many of the people I coach are unsure of what they want their lives to be like. They lack a clear understanding of their key principles and the influence they hope to achieve. I usually advise them to set aside some time for introspection. We frequently feel trapped when we don't know what we want, as Yogi Berra famously remarked, "If you don't know where you're going, you'll end up somewhere else." It's crucial to take the time to discover our strengths, interests, and objectives. Other individuals are frequently able to recognize these strengths. Someone once said that because I always liked to share my favorite applications with friends, I'd be good at teaching technology. I had no idea that fame would inspire me to cofound ReBoot Accel, a company that helps women adapt to the modern workplace. An excellent place to start is with our 2-page Personal Inventory. We want you to consider what energizes and depletes you, your peak experiences, your unwavering beliefs, and even how to create a personal vision statement for your life. Spend some time alone in seclusion, even for a short while. The time you take to reflect on yourself will be very beneficial to you.

Inertia

It might be challenging for many people to start something. While they are bursting with ideas, they find it difficult to start. My preferred advice is to divide a major activity into several smaller ones. Make manageable, tiny objectives for yourself, and treat yourself when you achieve them. then set out on your next objective. I enjoy challenging myself to cross off as many tasks from my to-do list in 30 minutes.

I treat myself to a delicious latte at my preferred coffee shop after finishing a chore I loathe. Also, I advise scheduling disciplined work time. Cal Newport discusses "deep work," or the job you perform when you're undistracted and highly concentrated. This job is planned and proactive rather than reactive (like checking emails). Unpleasant tasks are frequently scheduled into people's days as meetings with themselves. Choose when you are at your most energetic, and do the task then. The sensation of accomplishment may help you get through the remainder of the day, so checking off duties in the morning is frequently a smart idea. Who knows, maybe that initial success will give you the drive to take on yet another challenge!

Engage in the ONE YES challenge.
Try the ONE YES challenge during the coming week. See if you can force yourself to do anything that is much outside of your comfort zone by picking ONE tactic or obstacle. then consider how it performed. A fresh chance presented itself, perhaps? Did you learn a new talent or skill? Did you receive any praise for

your efforts? Did you discover anything you'll never do again? A growth mentality is all about trying new things, taking chances, and weighing the results, regardless of the outcome. You will gradually but certainly uncover a life of more joy, opportunities, and professional development by putting more emphasis on improving than demonstrating.